2019 SQA Past Papers with Answers

National 5
ENGLISH

2017, 2018 & 2019 Exams

HODDER GIBSON
AN HACHETTE UK COMPANY

This book contains the official SQA 2017, 2018 and 2019 Exams for National 5 English, with associated SQA-approved answers modified from the official marking instructions that accompany the paper. The 2016 RUAE paper has also been included to replace the 2019 RUAE paper, which cannot be reproduced for copyright reasons.

In addition the book contains study skills advice. This advice has been specially commissioned by Hodder Gibson, and has been written by experienced senior teachers and examiners in line with the new National 5 syllabus and assessment outlines. This is not SQA material but has been devised to provide further guidance for National 5 examinations.

Hodder Gibson is grateful to the copyright holders, as credited on the final page of the Answer section, for permission to use their material. Every effort has been made to trace the copyright holders and to obtain their permission for the use of copyright material. Hodder Gibson will be happy to receive information allowing us to rectify any error or omission in future editions.

Hachette UK's policy is to use papers that are natural, renewable and recyclable products and made from wood grown in well-managed forests and other controlled sources. The logging and manufacturing processes are expected to conform to the environmental regulations of the country of origin.

Orders: please contact Bookpoint Ltd, 130 Park Drive, Milton Park, Abingdon, Oxon OX14 4SE. Telephone: (44) 01235 827827. Fax: (44) 01235 400454. Lines are open 9.00–5.00, Monday to Friday, with a 24-hour message answering service. Visit our website at www.hoddereducation.co.uk. If you have queries or questions that aren't about an order, you can contact us at hoddergibson@hodder.co.uk

This collection first published in 2019 by
Hodder Gibson, an imprint of Hodder Education,
An Hachette UK Company
211 St Vincent Street
Glasgow G2 5QY

Typeset by Aptara, Inc.

Printed in the UK

A catalogue record for this title is available from the British Library

ISBN: 978-1-5104-7817-6

2 1

2020 2019

SCOTLAND EXCEL

We are an approved supplier on the Scotland Excel framework.

Schools can find us on their procurement system as:

Hodder & Stoughton Limited t/a Hodder Gibson.

MIX
Paper from responsible sources
FSC
www.fsc.org   FSC™ C104740

NATIONAL 5

2017

National
Qualifications
2017

X724/75/11

English
Reading for Understanding,
Analysis and Evaluation

FRIDAY, 12 MAY

9:00 AM – 10:00 AM

Total marks — 30

Attempt ALL questions.

Write your answers clearly in the answer booklet provided. In the answer booklet you must clearly identify the question number you are attempting.

Use **blue** or **black** ink.

Before leaving the examination room you must give your answer booklet to the Invigilator; if you do not, you may lose all the marks for this paper.

Resilience

My best friend, Mark, was a keen footballer. We played in my back garden every afternoon as kids, often down the local park, sometimes other kids would join us, and in the summer we never seemed to leave.

5   I often think of those long, endlessly absorbing days, game after game, sometimes until it got dark and we played by the dim glow of street lights. In the summer holidays, my mum would make a two-litre bottle of orange squash and we would pass it from player to player at half-time, none of us deterred by the fact it had got warm in the sun. My, it tasted good.

Mark never made it into the school team. He kept trying, kept going to the "trials", both at primary and senior school, but he was just off the pace. The disappointment was always bitter.
10 You could see it on his face. He yearned to play, to progress, to be able to read out a match report at school assembly (one of the honours of making the team). But he never did.

It has been reported that 98 per cent of those signed by English teams at 16 fail to make the transition into professional football. Many struggle to cope with rejection at such a tender age. Clinical psychologists report that many suffer anxiety, a loss of confidence and, in some cases,
15 depression. These youngsters are often described as being "left on football's scrapheap".

It seems to me, though, that the number rejected is, in fact, far higher. After all, the sifting process starts from the first time you kick a ball at the local park. I was one of the few who made it into my school team (I captained it). But when I went to trial for the district team, surrounded by the best players from all the schools in the area, the standard was high. Parents were
20 everywhere. I remember my heart beating out of my chest when the "scouts" arrived. I did not make it. I was crushed by the disappointment. How could it be otherwise? But I also realised that the race had only just started for those who had made the cut. Of those who made it into the district team, only a handful were picked by Reading, the local club. And of those who made it to Reading, only a fraction made it into professional football. Perhaps none made it all the way to
25 the top flight.

And that really is the point. When we watch any Premier League match, we are witnessing players who have made it through a filtering process of staggering dimensions. It is a process that does not merely discard 98 per cent of those who aspire, but something closer to 99·9999 per cent. For every first-team player, there are millions of others, like grains of sand on the beach, who have
30 tried, who have dreamt, but who have failed.

The majority, like Mark, never made it through the first lap. Others made it to the final straight, before dropping out. But this is football. This is life. Failure is an inevitable aspect of any competition worthy of the name. Without losers, there cannot be winners. Without pain, there cannot be joy. Without natural selection, there cannot be evolution. Failure is not the opposite of
35 progress; failure is part and parcel of progress.

Take a step back and you will see that football is a beautiful meritocracy. That so many dreams are shattered is testament to just how many dared to dream in the first place. The skills are transparent, the opportunities exist. There is no room for family favours or cosy alliances. The best of the best shine through, whether they are from a tough part of Liverpool, like Wayne
40 Rooney, or raised in grinding poverty in Uruguay, like Luis Suárez.

And the important point is that clubs have a responsibility to those who make it as far as the academies. They have a responsibility to create rounded people, with decent educations. Parents must support this approach, too, rather than exerting undue pressure on often vulnerable children. This is not just about giving youngsters a plan B; it is also about enlightened
45 self-interest.

Youngsters who are educated and self-assured are likely to be better footballers, too. The Ancient Greeks understood this only too well. They created strong links between the gymnasiums and the academies and embraced the humane idea that the mind and body grow together. The German football system has embraced this truth, too. The clubs there want intelligent and confident
50 young men. Such a cultural transformation needs to happen here, too. But I wish to make a deeper point. It is that we need to redefine our relationship with failure, not just in football but in life. We need to remind our children that losing is an essential (indeed, a beautiful) part of life. We need to emphasise the empowering idea that failure is less important, infinitely less so, than how we respond to it. Failing to make the grade at football is crushing. It is natural to be sad. But
55 it is also a pathway to a new reality.

Tens of thousands do not make it to Oxford or Cambridge. Hundreds of thousands of actors never win an Oscar. Tens of millions fail to make it into Manchester United or Chelsea. But this is not the end of life. It is merely the beginning. It is an opportunity to conceive a new dream, a new hope, a new way of finding meaning in this curious journey called life.

60 I often think about Mark. And I am thankful that his failures in football, so important, so trivial, never deterred him. He created new dreams, new aspirations, and lived a life that inspired all who knew him.

Life is too short, too precious, to be derailed by failure. We have to accept it. We have to embrace it.

Matthew Syed, in "The Times"

MARKS

Total marks — 30

Attempt ALL Questions

1. Look at lines 1—7, and explain how **one** example of the writer's word choice makes it clear that his memories of childhood football are positive.   2

2. Look at lines 8—11, and explain **in your own words** why Mark was so disappointed.

   You should make **four** key points in your answer.   4

3. Look at lines 12—25, and identify **in your own words six** points which the writer makes about young people hoping to become professional footballers.   6

4. Explain fully why the simile "like grains of sand on the beach" (line 29) is effective here.   2

5. Look at lines 31—35. By referring to **two** language features, explain how the writer makes clear his view about competition.

   You should refer to **two different** features such as word choice, imagery or sentence structure.   4

6. The writer tells us that "football is a beautiful meritocracy" (line 36).

   Explain **in your own words three** points the writer makes about merit being rewarded in the rest of this paragraph.   3

7. Look at lines 46—55, and identify, **in your own words** as far as possible, **five** points the writer makes in these lines about sport and/or life.   5

8. Look at lines 56—59, and explain how **one** feature of the writer's sentence structure is used to highlight an important point.   2

9. Select any expression in lines 60—64, and explain how it contributes to the passage's effective conclusion.   2

[END OF QUESTION PAPER]

National
Qualifications
2017

X724/75/12

English
Critical Reading

FRIDAY, 12 MAY
10:20 AM — 11:50 AM

Total marks — 40

SECTION 1 — Scottish Text — 20 marks

Read an extract from a Scottish text you have previously studied.

Choose ONE text from either

Part A — Drama   Pages 2—7

or

Part B — Prose   Pages 8—17

or

Part C — Poetry   Pages 18—25

Attempt ALL the questions for your chosen text.

SECTION 2 — Critical Essay — 20 marks

Attempt ONE question from the following genres — Drama, Prose, Poetry, Film and Television Drama, or Language.

Your answer must be on a different genre from that chosen in Section 1.

You should spend approximately 45 minutes on each Section.

Write your answers clearly in the answer booklet provided. In the answer booklet you must clearly identify the question number you are attempting.

Use **blue** or **black** ink.

Before leaving the examination room you must give your answer booklet to the Invigilator; if you do not, you may lose all the marks for this paper.

SECTION 1 — SCOTTISH TEXT — 20 marks

PART A — SCOTTISH TEXT — DRAMA

Text 1 — Drama

If you choose this text you may not attempt a question on Drama in Section 2.

Read the extract below and then attempt the following questions.

***Bold Girls* by Rona Munro**

Extract from Scene Two (The women are in a social club . . .)

	CASSIE:	It's the D.T.s.
	NORA:	It's the R.U.C.
	CASSIE:	Oh don't let it get to you.
	NORA:	So let's see your hand!
5		*Cassie holds hers out, it is also shaking*
	CASSIE:	It's our life style Mummy, we'll have to change our life style.
	NORA:	Is that right?
	CASSIE:	We're living too fast so we are, it's the same problem the film stars have, we'll burn ourselves out with all the excitement.
10	NORA:	Me and Joan Collins both.
	CASSIE:	You can write articles for the women's magazines, "Stop and Search, would your manicure stand up to the closest inspection?"
	NORA:	Let's see Marie's hand there.
		Marie is lost in her own thoughts
15		*Cassie pulls Marie's hand out, Nora and Cassie study it*
	CASSIE:	Steady as a rock.
	NORA:	Ah she's got a clear conscience.
	CASSIE:	Either that or she's in a coma, are you with us, Marie?
	MARIE:	Hmmm?
20	NORA:	Wired up but not plugged in.
	MARIE:	Are you reading my palm?
	CASSIE:	I will if you like.
		Deirdre approaches their table with a tray of drinks
		Cassie glances up at her, then bends theatrically over Marie's hand
25	CASSIE:	Oh, you're going to meet a dark stranger Marie, all in white but with a black wee heart. You better watch out for she'll thieve the clothes off your back but you'll not have peace till you nail the wee snake down and ask her what she's up to.

MARKS

30	DEIRDRE:	(*handing out the drinks correctly*) Black Russian — gin and lime — Pernod and blackcurrant.
	CASSIE:	So what about you Deirdre, if it is Deirdre?
	DEIRDRE:	It is.
	MARIE:	Cassie . . .
35	CASSIE:	I hope you've not taken a fancy to anything else that's caught your eye, like my handbag.
	DEIRDRE:	(*staring at Cassie for a minute*) It was in a car. A blue car.
	CASSIE:	What?
	DEIRDRE:	That I saw you before.
	CASSIE:	You're a lying hoor, you never saw anything.
40	DEIRDRE:	With a man. With him. With —

Cassie lunges at her before she can get another word out

Questions

1. Using your own words as far as possible, identify **four** things you learn about the women's lives in this extract.   **4**

2. Look at lines 1–12.

   Identify **one** example of humour and explain why it is effective.   **2**

3. Look at lines 13–35.

   (a) By referring to **one** example of word choice, explain how the playwright reveals the relationship between Nora and Marie.   **2**

   (b) By referring to **one** example of word choice, explain how the playwright reveals the relationship between Cassie and Deirdre.   **2**

4. Look at lines 36–41.

   By referring to **one** example of the writer's use of language, explain how this extract ends with a moment of tension.   **2**

5. By referring to this extract and to elsewhere in the play, show how mother and daughter-type relationships are explored.   **8**

[Turn over

OR

Text 2 — Drama

If you choose this text you may not attempt a question on Drama in Section 2.

Read the extract below and then attempt the following questions.

Sailmaker **by Alan Spence**

ALEC: What is it that gets intae ye? Wi the bettin ah mean?

DAVIE: Ah don't know. Just wan a these things.

    Ah suppose it's the feelin you've at least got a *chance*.

    Is there any wood in there? The paper just flares up then dies.

5   (*ALEC empties out contents of box, hands box to DAVIE*)

DAVIE: Great. (*Starts breaking up box, ALEC goes out, comes back with canvas tool-bag, cane bow. Fires imaginary arrow*) Bring me my bow of burning gold, eh?

    (*ALEC breaks bow for fire*)

    That's more like it. (*Warms himself*)

10   That's the stuff.

ALEC: (*Taking tools from canvas bag*) Look at this.

DAVIE: God. Ma auld sailmakin tools. (*Takes wooden marlinspike*) Ah was an apprentice when ah was your age. Hard work it wis tae.

    Ah worked on the Queen Mary ye know.

15   ALEC: Aye.

DAVIE: Worked on destroyers durin the War. Made gun-covers, awnings, tarpaulins.

    Made this wee bag!

ALEC: Did ye?

DAVIE: Oh aye. Used tae make leather wallets an things.

20   Made a shopping bag for yer mother. Made you a swing! Wi a big sorta bucket seat. Used tae hang it in the doorway there.

ALEC: Ah remember!

    You could still be makin things. Sellin them.

    (*DAVIE nods, shrugs*)

25   Could ye no go back tae yer trade?

DAVIE: Nae demand. Was different durin the War. They needed us then awright. Reserved occupation it was. Meant ah couldnae sign up. Been goin downhill since then but. Yards shuttin doon. Look at Harland's. Or where it was. Just a big empty space covered wi weeds.

30   Yer Uncle Billy had the right idea. Took his redundancy money and moved tae Aberdeen. Doin all right.

ALEC: Ian's an Aberdeen supporter now.

MARKS

DAVIE: Billy'll disown him for that!

ALEC: Did you ever think about movin?

35 DAVIE: Thought about it. (*Shrugs*) Thing is Billy bein a painter had more chance ae a job. Ah backed a loser right fae the start. Then it got even worse. They started bringin in aw the manmade fibres, usin machines. Got lassies daein hauf the work. Dead loss.

So for God's sake you dae somethin wi *your* life!

Questions

6. By referring to **two** examples from anywhere in this extract, explain how Alec's attitude towards Davie is revealed at this point in the play.   4

7. Look at lines 14—21.

By referring to **two** examples of language, explain how the writer suggests Davie's enthusiasm for his old trade.   4

8. Look at lines 26—38.

By referring to **two** examples of language, explain how the writer makes it clear that Davie's old trade is not important any more.   4

9. By referring to this extract and to elsewhere in the play, show how the character of Davie is presented.   8

[Turn over

OR

Text 3 — Drama

If you choose this text you may not attempt a question on Drama in Section 2.

Read the extract below and then attempt the following questions.

Tally's Blood **by Ann Marie Di Mambro**

	ROSINELLA:	You don't see it, do you? It's up to me to see everything.
	MASSIMO:	See what?
	ROSINELLA:	Why do you think she was in that state, eh?
	MASSIMO:	Over the wedding.
5	ROSINELLA:	Stupid eejit. Over Hughie, you mean.
	MASSIMO:	Hughie?
	ROSINELLA:	You no see the way he looks at our Lucia? He's crazy for her.
	MASSIMO:	Away you go. They grew up together.
	ROSINELLA:	She's to marry an Italian.
10	MASSIMO:	For God's sake, Rosie, she's no asking to marry him, just to go to his brother's wedding. You worry too much.
	ROSINELLA:	No, Massimo. I don't worry enough. It's been going on before my eyes and I've never seen it till tonight.
	MASSIMO:	Seen what?
15	ROSINELLA:	It's bad enough he's fell for her. But don't tell me she's to get falling for him. I'll soon put a stop to this before it starts.
	MASSIMO:	(*Groans*) Rosie . . .
20	ROSINELLA:	Italians are not interested in a lassie that's been out with anybody else — especially the Scotch men. They like a girl that's kept herself for them. I'm surprised at you.
	MASSIMO:	What have I done now?
	ROSINELLA:	Are you forgetting what this country did to the Italians during the war? (*Massimo groans*) They took you out of here as if you were a thief.
25	MASSIMO:	Listen, Rosie, all I care about the war is that it's over. I lost ma faither, ma brother and four years out ma life.
	ROSINELLA:	Well, I'll never get over it.
	MASSIMO:	Neither will I. But everybody suffered. Not just us.
	ROSINELLA:	Italians have got to stick together.
	MASSIMO:	Then come to Italy with me, Rosie, what do you say?
30		*Rosinella uncomfortable at mention of Italy.*
	ROSINELLA:	No . . . I don't think so.
	MASSIMO:	A wee holiday. The three of us.

MARKS

ROSINELLA:　Not yet, Massimo. You go, yourself. I don't mind.

35

MASSIMO:　Everybody was asking for you when I was over. Asking why you've never been back. Please, Rosie, I'm dying to show you my daddy's house. You can help me make it nice. Next year, maybe, eh? How about it, Rosie?

ROSINELLA:　I'm not going anywhere, Massimo, not until I see Lucia settled. (*A beat*) You think she's calmed down now? I think I'll take her to Glasgow on Saturday, go round the shops, get her something nice, take her to Palombo's to get her hair done. I'll go and tell her.

40

Questions

10.　Look at lines 1—17.

Using your own words as far as possible, identify the key areas of disagreement between Rosinella and Massimo. You should make **four** key points in your answer.　4

11.　Look at lines 9—20.

By referring to **two** examples of language, explain what is revealed about Rosinella's character.　4

12.　Look at lines 22—27.

By referring to **two** examples from their dialogue, explain how Rosinella and Massimo's different attitudes to the war are revealed.　4

13.　By referring to this extract and to elsewhere in the play, show how the character of Massimo is presented.　8

[Turn over

SECTION 1 — SCOTTISH TEXT — 20 marks

PART B — SCOTTISH TEXT — PROSE

Text 1 — Prose

If you choose this text you may not attempt a question on Prose in Section 2.

Read the extract below and then attempt the following questions.

The Cone-Gatherers **by Robin Jenkins**

In this extract from Chapter One, Duror is watching the cone-gatherers' hut.

The hut was lit by oil-lamp. He smelled paraffin as well as woodsmoke. He knew they picked up old cones to kindle the fire, and on Sunday they had worked for hours sawing up blown timber for firewood: they had been given permission to do so. The only window was not in the wall facing him, so that he could not see inside; but he had been in their hut so
5 often, they were in his imagination so vividly, and he was so close every sound they made could be interpreted; therefore it was easy for him to picture them as they went about making their meal. They peeled their potatoes the night before, and left them in a pot of cold water. They did not wash before they started to cook or eat. They did not change their clothes. They had no table; an upturned box did instead, with a newspaper for a
10 cloth; and each sat on his own bed. They seldom spoke. All evening they would be dumb, the taller brooding over a days-old paper, the dwarf carving some animal out of wood: at present he was making a squirrel. Seeing it half-finished that afternoon, holding it shudderingly in his hands, Duror had against his will, against indeed the whole frenzied thrust of his being, sensed the kinship between the carver and the creature whose likeness
15 he was carving. When complete, the squirrel would be not only recognisable, it would be almost alive. To Duror it had been the final defeat that such ability should be in a half-man, a freak, an imbecile. He had read that the Germans were putting idiots and cripples to death in gas chambers. Outwardly, as everybody expected, he condemned such barbarity; inwardly, thinking of idiocy and crippledness not as abstractions but as
20 embodied in the crouch-backed cone-gatherer, he had profoundly approved.

At last he roused himself and moved away. Yet, though he was going home, he felt he was leaving behind him in that hut something unresolved, which would never cease to torment him. It was almost as if there were not two brothers, but three; he himself was the third. Once he halted and looked back. His fists tightened on his gun. He saw himself returning,
25 kicking open the door, shouting at them his disgust, and then blasting them both to everlasting perdition. He felt an icy hand on his brow as he imagined that hideous but liberating fratricide.

MARKS

Questions

14.   Look at lines 1—12.

Using your own words as far as possible, identify **four** things we learn about how the cone-gatherers live.   4

15.   Look at lines 12—20.

By referring to **two** examples of language, explain how the writer makes clear Duror's feelings towards the cone-gatherers.   4

16.   Look at lines 21—27.

By referring to **two** examples of language, explain how Duror feels at this point.   4

17.   By referring to this extract and to elsewhere in the novel, show how the theme of good versus evil is explored.   8

[Turn over

OR

Text 2 — Prose

If you choose this text you may not attempt a question on Prose in Section 2.

Read the extract below and then attempt the following questions.

***The Testament of Gideon Mack* by James Robertson**

This extract is taken from the section of the novel where Gideon is relating his experience in the cave with the Devil after falling into the Black Jaws.

"You must understand," I said, "that I've never seriously thought you existed at all. It's a bit of a shock now, to find you just a few miles from Monimaskit."

"Don't think you're privileged," he said, sparking up a bit. "Don't think I'm paying you some kind of special attention. I do like Scotland, though, I spend a lot of time here. I once
5 preached to some women at North Berwick who thought they were witches. They were burnt for it, poor cows. I preached at Auchtermuchty another time, disguised as one of your lot, a minister, but the folk there found me out. Fifers, thrawn buggers, they were too sharp. But I do like Scotland. I like the miserable weather. I like the miserable people, the fatalism, the negativity, the violence that's always just below the surface. And I like the way
10 you deal with religion. One century you're up to your lugs in it, the next you're trading the whole apparatus in for Sunday superstores. Praise the Lord and thrash the bairns. Ask and ye shall have the door shut in your face. Blessed are they that shop on the Sabbath, for they shall get the best bargains. Oh, yes, this is a very fine country."

In spite of his claimed affection for Scotland, he seemed morose and fed up. Suddenly he
15 brightened.

"I know what I'll do if you want proof. I'll do what I said I would. I'll fix your leg."

This did not strike me as a good idea. "No," I said. "A surgeon should do that."

"Please," he said. "I'd like to."

When I said no again I heard a low rumble growl round the cave, which I took to be the
20 precursor of another stupendous roar. I made no further protest. He went over to the fire and I saw him put his right hand into the flames, deep into the middle of them. He was elbow-deep in fire but he didn't even flinch. His jacket didn't catch alight, and his hand and arm were quite unaffected by the heat. He stayed like that for fully three minutes. Then he turned and his whole arm was a white, pulsating glow. He came towards me and
25 reached for my leg with that terrible arm, and I shrank away from him.

"It doesn't hurt me," he said, "and it won't hurt you. Don't move."

I was too terrified to move. I was still clutching my mug of tea and he took it from me with his left hand and placed it on the ground. I closed my eyes and waited for the burning agony, but it did not come. I was aware only of a slight tingling sensation on my right thigh.
30 I opened my eyes and looked down. There was intense concentration on his face. His hand was *inside* my leg. Where the bone bulged out the skin was sizzling and popping like bacon in a pan, but there was no pain, only this faint tickle. He was pushing and prodding the bone back into place, welding it together. Smoke and steam issued from my leg, but still there was no pain. I felt only an incredible warmth, like the warmth of the spirit in his
35 black bottle, spreading through my whole body. His hand twisted something and my leg gave an involuntary jolt. "Don't move," he snapped. "I couldn't help it," I said.

MARKS

Questions

18. Look at lines 3—18.

Using your own words as far as possible, identify **three** things we learn about the Devil.

3

19. Look at lines 19—36.

By referring to **one** example, explain how language is used to show Gideon's fear.

2

20. Look again at lines 19—36.

Using your own words as far as possible, explain how the Devil fixes Gideon's leg. You should make **three** key points in your answer.

3

21. In this extract the devil's mood changes. By referring to **two** examples of language from anywhere in the extract, explain how the writer makes this clear.

4

22. By referring to this extract and to elsewhere in the novel, show how meeting the Devil affects the character of Gideon Mack.

8

[Turn over

OR

Text 3 — Prose

If you choose this text you may not attempt a question on Prose in Section 2.

Read the extract below and then attempt the following questions.

Kidnapped by Robert Louis Stevenson

In this extract from Chapter 20, David Balfour and Alan Breck Stewart are on the run after the killing of Red Fox.

The first peep of morning, then, showed us this horrible place, and I could see Alan knit his brow.

"This is no fit place for you and me," he said. "This is a place they're bound to watch."

And with that he ran harder than ever down to the water side, in a part where the river
5 was split in two among three rocks. It went through with a horrid thundering that made my belly quake; and there hung over the lynn a little mist of spray. Alan looked neither to the right nor to the left, but jumped clean upon the middle rock and fell there on his hands and knees to check himself, for that rock was small and he might have pitched over on the far side. I had scarce time to measure the distance or to understand the peril before I had
10 followed him, and he had caught and stopped me.

So there we stood, side by side upon a small rock slippery with spray, a far broader leap in front of us, and the river dinning upon all sides. When I saw where I was, there came on me a deadly sickness of fear, and I put my hand over my eyes. Alan took me and shook me; I saw he was speaking, but the roaring of the falls and the trouble of my mind prevented me
15 from hearing; only I saw his face was red with anger, and that he stamped upon the rock. The same look showed me the water raging by, and the mist hanging in the air: and with that I covered my eyes again and shuddered.

The next minute Alan had set the brandy bottle to my lips, and forced me to drink about a gill, which sent the blood into my head again. Then, putting his hands to his mouth and his
20 mouth to my ear, he shouted, "Hang or drown!" and turning his back upon me, leaped over the farther branch of the stream, and landed safe.

I was now alone upon the rock, which gave me the more room; the brandy was singing in my ears; I had this good example fresh before me, and just wit enough to see that if I did not leap at once, I should never leap at all. I bent low on my knees and flung myself forth,
25 with that kind of anger of despair that has sometimes stood me in stead of courage. Sure enough, it was but my hands that reached the full length; these slipped, caught again, slipped again; and I was sliddering back into the lynn, when Alan seized me, first by the hair, then by the collar, and with a great strain dragged me into safety.

Never a word he said, but set off running again for his life, and I must stagger to my feet
30 and run after him. I had been weary before, but now I was sick and bruised, and partly drunken with the brandy; I kept stumbling as I ran, I had a stitch that came near to overmaster me; and when at last Alan paused under a great rock that stood there among a number of others, it was none too soon for David Balfour.

MARKS

Questions

23. Using your own words as far as possible, summarise the main events in this extract. You should make **four** key points in your answer.

4

24. Look at lines 1—10.

    (a) Explain how **one** example of the writer's language shows that Alan is confident at this point in the extract.

2

    (b) Explain how **one** example of the writer's language shows how David feels at this point in the extract.

2

25. Look at lines 22—28.

    Explain how **one** example of sentence structure and **one** example of word choice contribute to the creation of drama at this point in the extract.

4

26. By referring to this extract and to elsewhere in the novel, show the ways in which Alan supports David physically **and/or** emotionally throughout the novel.

8

[Turn over

OR

Text 4 — Prose

If you choose this text you may not attempt a question on Prose in Section 2.

Read the extract below and then attempt the following questions.

The Crater **by Iain Crichton Smith**

On his hands and knees he squirmed forward, the others behind him. This was his first raid and he thought, "I am frightened." But it was different from being out in the open on a battlefield. It was an older fear, the fear of being buried in the earth, the fear of wandering through eternal passageways and meeting grey figures like weasels and fighting
5   with them in the darkness. He tested the wire. Thank God it had been cut. And then he thought, "Will we need the ladders?" The sides of the trenches were so deep sometimes that ladders were necessary to get out again. And as he crawled towards the German trenches he had a vision of Germans crawling beneath British trenches undermining them. A transparent imagined web hung below him in the darkness quivering with grey spiders.

10   He looked at his illuminated watch. The time was right. Then they were in the German trenches. The rest was a series of thrustings and flashes. Once he thought he saw or imagined he saw from outside a dugout a man sitting inside reading a book. It was like looking through a train window into a house before the house disappears. There were Mills bombs, hackings of bayonets, scurryings and breathings as of rats. A white face towered
15   above him, his pistol exploded and the face disappeared. There was a terrible stink all around him, and the flowing of blood. Then there was a long silence. Back. They must get back. He passed the order along. And then they wriggled back again avoiding the craters which lay around them, created by shells, and which were full of slimy water. If they fell into one of these they would be drowned. As he looked, shells began to fall into them
20   sending up huge spouts of water. Over the parapet. They were over the parapet. Crouched they had run and scrambled and were over. Two of them were carrying a third. They stumbled down the trench. There were more wounded than he had thought. Wright . . . one arm seemed to have been shot off. Sergeant Smith was bending over him. "You'll get sent home all right," he was saying. Some of the men were tugging at their equipment and
25   talking feverishly. Young Ellis was lying down, blood pouring from his mouth. Harris said, "Morrison's in the crater."

He and Sergeant Smith looked at each other. They were both thinking the same: there is no point, he's had it. They could see each other's eyes glaring whitely through the black, but could not tell the expression on the faces. The shells were still falling, drumming and
30   shaking the earth. All these craters out there, these dead moons.

MARKS

Questions

27. Look at lines 1—9.

    By referring to **two** examples, explain how the writer's use of language makes clear the soldier's fear.

    4

28. Look at lines 11—16 ("The rest . . . flowing of blood").

    Using your own words as far as possible, identify **four** ways in which the trenches are horrific.

    4

29. Look at lines 16—21 ("Back . . . and were over").

    By referring to **one** example, explain how the sentence structure highlights the danger faced by the men.

    2

30. Look at lines 27—30.

    By referring to **one** example, explain how the writer's use of language creates a sense of despair.

    2

31. By referring to this extract and to at least one other story by Crichton Smith, show how he uses word choice **and/or** symbolism to highlight an important message.

    8

[Turn over

OR

Text 5 — Prose

If you choose this text you may not attempt a question on Prose in Section 2.

Read the extract below and then attempt the following questions.

Zimmerobics **by Anne Donovan**

So that was that. At 11am I assembled with the others in the dayroom. I knew most of their faces, but was surprised to see some of them wearing tracksuits and trainers. It hadn't occurred to me to ask what to wear and I didn't possess such things anyway, but somehow I felt out of place. It was like starting school and discovering that the others were wearing
5   school uniform and you weren't.

Cheryl bounced into the room, wearing a pair of trainers that made her feet look like a horse's hooves. Her hair was tied back with an emerald green band which matched her shimmering leotard and tights.

"I hope she doesn't need to go to the toilet in a hurry," muttered a voice behind me.

10   "Hi there. It's great to see so many of you here this morning. Now, take it at your own pace and if you feel uncomfortable or out of breath any time, stop for a wee rest. Enjoy!"

She switched on the music. We stood behind our Zimmers as she got us to stretch first one, then the other, arm, move our heads to each side, then stretch our legs. I heard a few creaking sounds but so far so good. We moved on to circling movements and, as the record
15   progressed, I felt an unaccustomed but pleasant tingling in my limbs.

"That was the warm-up. The next one's a bit faster."

The next record was a catchy tune about living in the YMCA. I couldn't keep up with the routine at first but, once we'd been through it a few times, I became quite proficient. We had to raise our right then our left arms to the Y and the M, then pause on the C and hold
20   our Zimmers as we bent both legs for the A. Then we marched (well, shuffled in most cases) round to the left, raised our left arms twice to the Y and the M (that was a bit tricky), paused at the C and kicked our left leg out to the A. During the verse we did some marching and a few kicks, then we repeated the chorus routine, this time moving to the right. At the end we clapped three times, boldly taking both hands off our Zimmer frames.

25   It was brilliant. I hadn't felt like this for years. My body was old and decrepit, but it still worked. I had been concentrating so hard on what I was doing I had forgotten the others, but now I looked round and saw their faces, flushed and smiling.

"You all did great. Give yourselves a round of applause." She clapped her hands above her head while we patted our hands together, slightly embarrassed.

30   "Same time next week," she called as we hirpled out of the dayroom, old once again.

The memory of the exercise class lingered on for the rest of the day, not just in my mind as I relived the routine, but in my bones and muscles. I thought I'd be sore and stiff but, surprisingly, I felt better, as though someone had oiled all the creaky old joints. There was a feeling in them which I suppose you would call an ache, but it was a pleasant ache, an
35   ache of life.

MARKS

Questions

32. Using your own words as far as possible, explain how Miss Knight's attitude to Zimmerobics changes over the extract. You should make **two** key points in your answer.

2

33. Look at lines 12—35.

    By referring to **one** example, explain how the writer's use of language makes clear the problems associated with old age.

2

34. Look again at lines 12—35.

    By referring to **two** examples, explain how the writer's use of language makes clear Miss Knight's feelings about exercise.

4

35. Look at the extract as a whole.

    By referring to **two** examples, explain how the writer's use of language creates humour.

4

36. By referring to this extract and to at least one other story, show how Donovan creates convincing characters.

8

[Turn over

SECTION 1 — SCOTTISH TEXT — 20 marks

PART C — SCOTTISH TEXT — POETRY

Text 1 — Poetry

If you choose this text you may not attempt a question on Poetry in Section 2.

Read the poem below and then attempt the following questions.

War Photographer by Carol Ann Duffy

In his darkroom he is finally alone
with spools of suffering set out in ordered rows.
The only light is red and softly glows,
as though this were a church and he
5   a priest preparing to intone a Mass.
Belfast. Beirut. Phnom Penh. All flesh is grass.

He has a job to do. Solutions slop in trays
beneath his hands, which did not tremble then
though seem to now. Rural England. Home again
10   to ordinary pain which simple weather can dispel,
to fields which don't explode beneath the feet
of running children in a nightmare heat.

Something is happening. A stranger's features
faintly start to twist before his eyes,
15   a half-formed ghost. He remembers the cries
of this man's wife, how he sought approval
without words to do what someone must
and how the blood stained into foreign dust.

A hundred agonies in black and white
20   from which his editor will pick out five or six
for Sunday's supplement. The reader's eyeballs prick
with tears between the bath and pre-lunch beers.
From the aeroplane he stares impassively at where
he earns his living and they do not care.

MARKS

Questions

37. Look at lines 1—6.

    By referring to **one** example of word choice, explain how the poet suggests that the war photographer is like "a priest" in "church".   2

38. Look at lines 9—12.

    By referring to **two** examples of language, explain how the poet makes it clear that the war photographer's home country is very different from the countries he visits.   4

39. Look at lines 13—18.

    By referring to **two** examples of language, explain how the poet makes it clear that the war photographer has been strongly affected by his experiences.   4

40. Look at lines 19—24.

    Using your own words as far as possible, explain **two** key ideas explored in the final stanza.   2

41. By referring to this poem and to at least one other by Duffy, show how the idea of people suffering painful experiences is a feature of her poetry.   8

[Turn over

OR

Text 2 — Poetry

If you choose this text you may not attempt a question on Poetry in Section 2.

Read the poem below and then attempt the following questions.

Trio by Edwin Morgan

Coming up Buchanan Street, quickly, on a sharp winter evening
a young man and two girls, under the Christmas lights —
The young man carries a new guitar in his arms,
the girl on the inside carries a very young baby,
5   and the girl on the outside carries a chihuahua.
And the three of them are laughing, their breath rises
in a cloud of happiness, and as they pass
the boy says, 'Wait till he sees this but!'
The chihuahua has a tiny Royal Stewart tartan coat like a teapot-
10   holder,
the baby in its white shawl is all bright eyes and mouth like favours
     in a fresh sweet cake,
the guitar swells out under its milky plastic cover, tied at the neck
     with silver tinsel tape and a brisk sprig of mistletoe.
15   Orphean sprig! Melting baby! Warm chihuahua!
The vale of tears is powerless before you.
Whether Christ is born, or is not born, you
put paid to fate, it abdicates
                 under the Christmas lights.
20   Monsters of the year
go blank, are scattered back,
can't bear this march of three.

    —And the three have passed, vanished in the crowd
(yet not vanished, for in their arms they wind
25   the life of men and beasts, and music,
laughter ringing them round like a guard)
at the end of this winter's day.

MARKS

Questions

42. Look at lines 1—8.

    By referring to **one** example of language, explain how the poet creates a sense of joy.   2

43. Look at lines 11—14.

    By referring to **one** example of language, explain how the poet suggests the idea of innocence.   2

44. Look at lines 15—22.

    By referring to **two** examples of language, explain how the poet makes it clear that the group of three represents a strong force.   4

45. Look at lines 23—27.

    By referring to **two** examples of language, explain how the poet creates a positive ending to the poem.   4

46. By referring to this poem and to at least one other by Morgan, show how setting is an important feature of his poetry.   8

[Turn over

OR

Text 3 — Poetry

If you choose this text you may not attempt a question on Poetry in Section 2.

Read the poem below and then attempt the following questions.

Aunt Julia **by Norman MacCaig**

Aunt Julia spoke Gaelic
very loud and very fast.
I could not answer her —
I could not understand her.

5   She wore men's boots
when she wore any.
— I can see her strong foot,
stained with peat,
paddling with the treadle of the spinningwheel
10 while her right hand drew yarn
marvellously out of the air.

Hers was the only house
where I've lain at night
in the absolute darkness
15 of a box bed, listening to
crickets being friendly.

She was buckets
and water flouncing into them.
She was winds pouring wetly
20 round house-ends.
She was brown eggs, black skirts
and a keeper of threepennybits
in a teapot.

Aunt Julia spoke Gaelic
25 very loud and very fast.
By the time I had learned
a little, she lay
silenced in the absolute black
of a sandy grave
30 at Luskentyre. But I hear her still, welcoming me
with a seagull's voice
across a hundred yards
of peatscrapes and lazybeds
and getting angry, getting angry
35 with so many questions
unanswered.

MARKS

Questions

47. Look at lines 1—4.

    By referring to **one** example of language, explain how the poet creates a clear sense of frustration.

    2

48. Look at lines 5—23.

    By referring to **two** examples of language, explain how the poet makes clear what Aunt Julia represents.

    4

49. Look at lines 26—30 ("By the . . . Luskentyre").

    By referring to **two** examples of language, explain how the poet creates a sad tone.

    4

50. Look at lines 30—36 ("But I . . . unanswered").

    How effective do you find these lines as a conclusion to the poem? You should refer to **one** example from these lines, and to the language **and/or** ideas of the rest of the poem.

    2

51. By referring to this poem and to at least one other by MacCaig, show how being separated from people **and/or** things is an important idea in his poetry.

    8

[Turn over

OR

Text 4 — Poetry

If you choose this text you may not attempt a question on Poetry in Section 2.

Read the poem below and then attempt the following questions.

Bed by Jackie Kay

She is that guid tae me so she is
an Am a burden tae her, I know Am ur.
Stuck here in this big blastit bed
year in, year oot, ony saint wuid complain.

5   There's things she has tae dae fir me
A' wish she didnae huv tae dae.
Am her wean noo, wey ma great tent o' nappy,
an champed egg in a cup, an mashed tattie.

Aw the treats A' used tae gie her,
10 she's gieing me. A' dinny ken whit happened.
We dinny talk any mair. Whether it's jist
the blethers ha been plucked oot o' us

an Am here like some skinny chicken,
ma skin aw bubbles and dots and spots,
15 loose flap noo (an yet as a young wuman
A' took pride in ma guid smooth skin.)

Aw A' dae is sit an look oot this windae.
A've seen hale generations graw up
an simmer doon fray this same windae —
20 that's no seen a lick o' paint fir donkeys.

The Kerrs have disappeared, but the last
Campbells ur still here so Am telt —
tho' hauf the time A' dinny believe her:
A've no seen ony Campbell in a lang time.

25 My dochter says 'Awright mother?'
haunds me a thin broth or puried neep
an A say 'Aye fine,' an canny help
the great heaving sigh that comes oot

my auld loose lips, nor ma crabbit tut,
30 nor ma froon when A' pu' ma cardie tight
aroon ma shooders fir the night drawin in.
Am jist biding time so am ur.

Time is whit A' hauld between
the soft bits o' ma thumbs,
35 the skeleton underneath ma night goon;
aw the while the glaring selfish moon

lights up this drab wee prison.
A'll be gone and how wull she feel?
No that Am saying A' want her guilty.
40 No that Am saying Am no grateful.

Page twenty-four

MARKS

Questions

52. Look at lines 1—12.

By referring to **two** examples of language, explain how the poet makes it clear that the speaker is unhappy with her current situation.

4

53. Look at lines 13—20.

By referring to **two** examples of language, explain how the poet gives a clear impression of the negative aspects of old age.

4

54. Look at lines 21—31.

By referring to **one** example of language, explain how the poet suggests that the speaker's relationship with her daughter is problematic.

2

55. Look at lines 32—40.

Using your own words as far as possible, explain the speaker's thoughts about what her life has become. You should make **two** key points in your answer.

2

56. By referring to this poem and to at least one other by Kay, show how she explores important changes in people's lives.

8

[END OF SECTION 1]

[Turn over

SECTION 2 — CRITICAL ESSAY — 20 marks

Attempt ONE question from the following genres — Drama, Prose, Poetry, Film and Television Drama, or Language.

Your answer must be on a different genre from that chosen in Section 1.

You should spend approximately 45 minutes on this Section.

DRAMA

Answers to questions in this part should refer to the text and to such relevant features as characterisation, key scene(s), structure, climax, theme, plot, conflict, setting . . .

1. Choose a play in which there is conflict.

   Describe the conflict and by referring to the playwright's use of dramatic techniques, explain fully how the conflict develops.

2. Choose a play in which there is a scene that can be described as a turning point.

   Briefly describe what happens in this scene, and by referring to appropriate dramatic techniques, go on to explain why the scene is important to the play as a whole.

PROSE

Answers to questions in this part should refer to the text and to such relevant features as characterisation, setting, language, key incident(s), climax, turning point, plot, structure, narrative technique, theme, ideas, description . . .

3. Choose a novel **or** a short story **or** a work of non-fiction which deals with an important issue or theme.

   By referring to appropriate techniques, show how the issue or theme is explored.

4. Choose a novel **or** a short story **or** a work of non-fiction which has a memorable character/person, place or event.

   By referring to appropriate techniques, explain how the writer makes the character/person, place or event memorable.

POETRY

> *Answers to questions in this part should refer to the text and to such relevant features as word choice, tone, imagery, structure, content, rhythm, rhyme, theme, sound, ideas . . .*

5. Choose a poem which has a strong message.

   Consider the whole poem, and by referring to poetic techniques explain how the strong message is explored.

6. Choose a poem which creates a particular mood or atmosphere.

   By referring to poetic techniques, show how the poet creates this particular mood or atmosphere.

FILM AND TELEVISION DRAMA

> *Answers to questions in this part should refer to the text and to such relevant features as use of camera, key sequence, characterisation, mise-en-scène, editing, setting, music/sound, special effects, plot, dialogue . . .*

7. Choose a scene or a sequence from a film or TV drama* which has a powerful impact on the audience.

   By referring to appropriate techniques, explain how the director creates this impact.

8. Choose a film or TV drama* which explores an important issue.

   By referring to appropriate techniques, explain how the director presents the issue in the film/TV drama as a whole.

* "TV drama" includes a single play, a series or a serial.

[Turn over

LANGUAGE

> *Answers to questions in this part should refer to the text and to such relevant features as register, accent, dialect, slang, jargon, vocabulary, tone, abbreviation . . .*

9. Consider the use of persuasive language in one or more advertisements that you have studied.

    By referring to appropriate language techniques, explain how language is used effectively.

10. Consider the language used by two groups of people who are different in an important way. For example, they may be different in age, be from different places, or have different jobs.

    By referring to specific examples, explain how language differences are important.

[END OF SECTION 2]

[END OF QUESTION PAPER]

NATIONAL 5

2018

National Qualifications 2018

X824/75/11

English
Reading for Understanding, Analysis and Evaluation

MONDAY, 14 MAY

9:00 AM – 10:00 AM

Total marks — 30

Attempt ALL questions.

Write your answers clearly in the answer booklet provided. In the answer booklet you must clearly identify the question number you are attempting.

Use **blue** or **black** ink.

Before leaving the examination room you must give your answer booklet to the Invigilator; if you do not you may lose all the marks for this paper.

Why do cats love bookshops?

When I walk into my local bookshop, the first thing I do (after saying hi to the owners) is look for the shop cat, Tiny the Mini Master. Tiny is the photogenic spirit of the place who gives you approximately five seconds to impress him, otherwise he goes right back to sleep on that pile of nineteenth-century novels.

5 I understand the idea of people being either more for dogs or cats, I do. I also get the weird looks I've received for proudly stating that I'm for both, that I can relate to dogs and their wonderfully dumb, but fiercely loyal attitudes, as well as appreciate the way cats keep you in check by making you work for their love. But I can say without any doubt that bookshop cats represent the apex of domesticated pets.

10 If a bookshop is so fortunate as to have a cat on the premises during opening hours, you can bet that feline is co-owner, manager, security, and the abiding conscience of the place. Cats generally seem above it all — that's what I tend to like about them. Personally, I'm more like a dog, all stupid and excited about the smallest things, easy to read and always hungry. Cats, on the other hand, look right through you, force you to contemplate things; they just seem smarter than 15 they're letting on, as if they know everything but won't tell. So it makes sense to see so many of them navigating the stacks of dusty old hardcovers at used bookshops. But there's another, deeper reason cats make so much sense in bookshops — it's in their DNA.

'One cannot help wondering what the silent critic on the hearth-rug thinks of our strange conventions — the mystic Persian, whose ancestors were worshipped as gods, whilst we, their 20 masters and mistresses, grovelled in caves and painted our bodies blue,' the famous novelist Virginia Woolf wrote in the essay 'On a Faithful Friend'. Cats held a special place in ancient Egyptian society, to the point where if you even accidentally killed a cat, you'd be sentenced to death. Cats were often adorned with jewels, and fed meals that would make today's tinned cat food look like, well, tinned cat food. They were sometimes mummified (the grieving owners 25 shaved off their eyebrows as an act of mourning). Bastet, the deity representing protection, fertility, and motherhood, could turn herself into a cat, hence the popular idea that Egyptians worshipped them.

It's pretty obvious that cats haven't really moved on from the sort of treatment they received in the time of Pharaoh. They carry themselves in a stately manner and demand that you treat them 30 with a certain amount of reverence, letting you know if you're doing a good job of petting them, when they're ready for their meal, and making you aware of what they like and what displeases them. My cats certainly do. They love their comfy spots, and often give me a hard time when I try to make them move, shooting me a look, letting out a sad meow, and then instigating a showdown which almost always ends with me picking them up. And their favourite place in my 35 house? Among my books.

Egypt, where cats are believed to have been first domesticated, is also where the relationship with bookshops can be traced. While mainly used to keep rodents away from homes and crops, cats were trained to keep pests away from papyrus rolls which contained texts. Without cats, in fact, it's hard to imagine how Egyptian civilisation could have so successfully weathered the 40 diseases and famine caused by vermin — but also imagine the knowledge that might have been lost were it not for those four-legged protectors guarding the temples from tiny intruders.

Today, when we think of a cat chasing a mouse it's usually in some cartoonesque, Tom and Jerry sort of way. The dumb cat is always foiled by its tiny adversary, like we're supposed to forgive the little pests for gnawing on our possessions and spreading disease. It's unfair.

45　So how did they end up in bookshops? Look to Russia and a decree issued by Empress Elizabeth in 1745 for the 'best and biggest cats, capable of catching mice' to be sent to the Museum of St Petersburg to protect the treasures contained within from rats (the tradition lives on to the present day, with dozens of strays living in the basement of the museum). Not long after, in the early 1800s, with Europeans still sure that rats caused the Black Death (this idea has been recently
50　debunked, with scholars now believing that giant gerbils might be to blame), and rat catchers unable to stop rodents from overrunning filthy urban centres, the British government started to encourage libraries to keep cats in order to bring down populations of book-loving vermin. It made sense that bookshop owners would also employ the four-legged security guards to keep their shops free of pests. Cats were easy to find, and all you had to do was feed them as
55　compensation. And once cats were invited into bookshops, they never really left.

Cats are quiet and want to be left alone for the bulk of the day; they're animals that long for solitude, much like readers and writers. It began as a working relationship, but became something more than that, something deeper. Cats ultimately became integral to the bookshop experience, a small part of why you would rather go to your local shop than buy online. Sure, not every
60　bookshop has a cat prowling around; but in the ones that do, the cats are a big part of what makes these stores great (along with, you know, the booksellers and the comfortable places to sit and read).

Of course, if you asked a cat, he'd say he was the main attraction, but that's what you get from a species which once reached god-like status.

Jason Diamond, Literary Hub

Total marks — 30

Attempt ALL Questions

1. Look at lines 1—4. Explain **in your own words** why 'the first thing' the writer does when he visits his local bookshop is to 'look for the shop cat, Tiny.'

   You should make **two** key points in your answer.

   2

2. Look at lines 5—17. Identify, **in your own words** as far as possible, **five** positive points the writer makes about cats.

   5

3. Look at lines 18—27. Identify, **in your own words** as far as possible, **four** ways in which cats 'held a special place' in the ancient world.

   4

4. By referring to the sentence in lines 28—29 ('It's pretty obvious . . . of Pharaoh'), explain how it helps to provide a link between the writer's ideas at this point in the passage.

   2

5. Look at lines 32—35 ('My cats . . . my books.'). Explain how **one** example of the writer's use of sentence structure makes it clear what cats prefer.

   2

6. Look at lines 36—41. Explain how **two** examples of the writer's word choice makes it clear that cats played a very important part in preserving Egyptian writing.

   4

7. Look at lines 42—44. Explain how **two** examples of language make it clear that the writer is defending cats here.

   4

8. Look at lines 45—55. Summarise, **in your own words** as far as possible, how cats ended up in bookshops.

   You should make **five** key points in your answer.

   5

9. Look at lines 56—64. Select any expression from these lines and explain how it contributes to the passage's effective conclusion.

   2

[END OF QUESTION PAPER]

National Qualifications 2018

X824/75/12

English Critical Reading

MONDAY, 14 MAY

10:20 AM – 11:50 AM

Total marks — 40

SECTION 1 — Scottish Text — 20 marks

Read an extract from a Scottish text you have previously studied.

Choose ONE text from either

Part A — Drama   Pages 2–7
or
Part B — Prose   Pages 8–17
or
Part C — Poetry   Pages 18–25

Attempt ALL the questions for your chosen text.

SECTION 2 — Critical Essay — 20 marks

Attempt ONE question from the following genres — Drama, Prose, Poetry, Film and Television Drama, or Language.

Your answer must be on a different genre from that chosen in Section 1.

You should spend approximately 45 minutes on each Section.

Write your answers clearly in the answer booklet provided. In the answer booklet you must clearly identify the question number you are attempting.

Use **blue** or **black** ink.

Before leaving the examination room you must give your answer booklet to the Invigilator; if you do not, you may lose all the marks for this paper.

SECTION 1 — SCOTTISH TEXT — 20 marks

PART A — SCOTTISH TEXT — DRAMA

Text 1 — Drama

If you choose this text you may not attempt a question on Drama in Section 2.

Read the extract below and then attempt the following questions.

Bold Girls by Rona Munro

In this extract, Cassie, Marie and Nora have returned from their night out. They are in Marie's house discussing the events of the night.

NORA: (*drawing herself up*) Oh you'll be telling me a different tale in the morning! There's no end to your wild tales, Cassie! There's no end to them, Marie! (*She snatches up her drink and takes an angry gulp*) And I'd it all to do. I'd it all to put up with! Are you hearing me?

5   *Cassie doesn't look at Nora*

         (*Taking another gulp*) He's lost my remnant, Marie. He's lost it. I'd all the money saved, as good as paid. It's gone he says, gone. I'll never find a colour like that again. Months I'd been dreaming of the glow that would give my front room. Months. And he's lost it. I'll never have it the way I want it now. Never. (*She is*
10   *getting tearful in her turn*) My lovely wee room. It could be lovely, couldn't it, Marie?

MARIE: You'll get it right, Nora.

NORA: Well where will I ever find a colour like that again? Tell me that? (*Waiting for a response*) Cassie? I'm asking you!

15   CASSIE: (*looking up at Nora*) Good night, Mummy.

Nora stares at her for a moment, then she nods

NORA: Well I'm going up the town tomorrow. I'm just going to go up the town and buy a piece of what I want. I'll get credit. I'll give them a false address and I'll get credit and I'll have my loose covers. And if you don't want to come and help
20   choose them, Cassie, you needn't sit on them.

Nora exits

Marie puts the gin bottle down in front of Cassie. Cassie helps herself to another drink

MARIE: (*quietly*) It'll tear the heart out of her, Cassie.

CASSIE: Mummy's heart is made of steel. She had to grow it that way.

25   *Marie reaches over and takes Michael's picture. She goes and rehangs it carefully*

         There's a waitress up that club will be walking round without her hair tomorrow if I can find her.

MARIE: You don't know it was her. There's people in and out of here all the time.

CASSIE: Who else would it be?

MARKS

30 MARIE: Well — if she's thieving round the club there'll be others sort her out before you do. (*She steps back to admire the picture*)

CASSIE: How do you stand it here, Marie?

MARIE: Sure where else would I go?

CASSIE: How do you keep that smile on your face?

35 MARIE: Super-glue.

CASSIE: There's not one piece of bitterness in you, is there?

MARIE: Oh Cassie.

CASSIE: You see, you're good. And I'm just wicked.

MARIE: Aye you're a bold woman altogether.

40 CASSIE: Is it hard being good?

MARIE: I took lessons.

Questions

1. Using your own words as far as possible, identify **four** things we learn about the main characters in this extract.   4

2. Look at lines 6—11.

    By referring to **two** examples of language, explain how the writer makes it clear that Nora is upset.   4

3. By referring to **two** examples from anywhere in this extract, explain how stage directions are used to create tension between characters.   4

4. By referring to this extract and to elsewhere in the play, show how the main characters are presented as being 'Bold Girls'.   8

[Turn over

OR

Text 2 — Drama

If you choose this text you may not attempt a question on Drama in Section 2.

Read the extract below and then attempt the following questions.

Sailmaker **by Alan Spence**

BILLY: Ah hear the boy's daein well at school.

DAVIE: Oh aye. He's clever. He'll get on.

BILLY: He'll get on a lot better if you screw the heid, right?

DAVIE: C'mon Billy, ah dae ma best. It's just . . .

5 BILLY: Ah know it's hard on yer own an that . . .

DAVIE: Naw ye don't know. Naebody knows, unless they've been through it. (*Quieter*) Comin hame's the worst. The boy's oot playin. Hoose is empty. Gets on top of ye.

        The other night there, ah got this queer feelin. Ah felt as if aw the furniture an everythin was *watching* me. Sounds daft, eh? Maybe ah'm goin aff ma heid!

10 BILLY: Bound tae take a while tae get over it.

DAVIE: If ah ever dae.

(*They cross to where* ALEC *is playing with yacht*)

BILLY: (To ALEC) How ye doin wee yin? What's this ye've got? (*Picks up yacht*)

ALEC: Used tae be Jackie's.

15 DAVIE: Ah'm gonnae fix it up, when ah've got the time.

ALEC: Ye've been sayin that for weeks!

BILLY: Ah could paint it if ye like.

ALEC: Would ye?

BILLY: Aye, sure. Should come up really nice. Ah'll take it away wi me. Get it done this
20   week.

ALEC: This week!

BILLY: Nae bother.

ALEC: What colours will ye make it?

BILLY: Ah think the hull has tae be white. Ah've got a nice white gloss at work. The keel
25   ah could dae in blue. Maybe put a wee blue rim round the edge here. An ah think
        ah've got a light brown that would do just fine for the deck. That suit ye awright?

ALEC: Great!

BILLY: Ye won't even recognise it. It'll be like a brand new boat.

ALEC: It'll be dead real, eh?

30 BILLY: It'll be that real we can aw sail away in it!

MARKS

DAVIE: Away tae Never Never Land!

BILLY: Right, ah'll be seein ye.

(*Takes yacht, exits*)

Questions

5. Look at lines 1—11.

   By referring to **two** examples of language, explain how the writer makes it clear that Davie is having a difficult time.

   4

6. Look at lines 13—28.

   By referring to **two** examples of language, explain what we learn about Billy's character.

   4

7. Look at lines 29—33.

   By referring to **one** example, explain how either Alec **or** Davie react to Billy's promise of fixing the yacht.

   2

8. Using your own words as far as possible, explain why the yacht is important in this extract. You should make **two** key points.

   2

9. By referring to this extract and to elsewhere in the play, show how family relationships are explored.

   8

[Turn over

OR

Text 3 — Drama

If you choose this text you may not attempt a question on Drama in Section 2.

Read the extract below and then attempt the following questions.

Tally's Blood **by Ann Marie Di Mambro**

	ROSINELLA:	You better watch these lassies. (*Franco scoffs*) Who is it anyway? Anybody I know?
	FRANCO:	(*Face lights up talking about her*) This is not 'anybody'. It's Bridget Devlin. You know her?
5	ROSINELLA:	(*Disapproving*) From the Auld Toon? Adam Devlin's lassie?
	FRANCO:	What if she is?
	ROSINELLA:	No harm to the lassie, Franco, but look at that family. Must be six or seven weans.
	FRANCO:	Eight.
10	ROSINELLA:	(*Shocked*) Eight weans! She keeps having them and she cannie even look after them right. And look at me! It's no fair, is it. Twelve years I've been married — and nothing. Me an Italian as well.
	FRANCO:	They're a great family, Rosinella. Really close.
	ROSINELLA:	You never met anybody in Italy?
15	FRANCO:	I wasn't looking.
	ROSINELLA:	I says to Massimo, I wouldn't be surprised if you come back engaged.
	FRANCO:	I told you, Rosinella, I've got someone.
	ROSINELLA:	You're surely no keen on this Scotch girl?
	FRANCO:	What if I am?
20	ROSINELLA:	Then she must be giving you something you can't get from an Italian girl. I'm telling you, you better watch yourself.
	FRANCO:	You know nothing about Bridget.
25	ROSINELLA:	Now you listen good to me, son. These Scotch girls, they're all the same. They just go out with you for one thing. Because your faither's got a shop and they think you've got money.
	FRANCO:	(*Indignant*) Thanks very much.
	ROSINELLA:	Alright. Alright. And because you're tall . . .
	FRANCO:	Good looking . . .
	ROSINELLA:	You're good fun to be with . . .
30	FRANCO:	. . . a good kisser, a good dancer . . .
	ROSINELLA:	Aye, but that's because you're Italian.

MARKS

FRANCO: Oh, they like that alright. All I have to do is say 'Ciao Bella' and they're all over me.

Lucia in from front shop.

35   Ciao Bella.

She jumps on his back for a piggyback.

See what I mean?

ROSINELLA: Listen — these girls. (*Lowers voice so Lucia won't hear*) Don't think I don't understand. You're no different from all the other Italian men. You're young,
40   you've got the warm blood. But it's one thing to play around with them, so long as you marry your own kind. You watch none of them catches you. That's the kind of thing they do here.

Questions

10.   Look at lines 1—6.

By referring to **two** examples of language, explain how the writer makes it clear that there is conflict between Franco and Rosinella.   4

11.   Look at lines 7—13.

(a)   By referring to **one** example, explain how the writer demonstrates Rosinella's opinion of Bridget's family.   2

(b)   By referring to **one** example, explain how the writer demonstrates Franco's opinion of Bridget's family.   2

12.   Look at lines 15—42.

By referring to **two** examples of language, explain what is revealed about Franco's character.   4

13.   By referring to this extract and to elsewhere in the play, show how the character of Rosinella is presented.   8

[Turn over

SECTION 1 — SCOTTISH TEXT — 20 marks

PART B — SCOTTISH TEXT — PROSE

Text 1 — Prose

If you choose this text you may not attempt a question on Prose in Section 2.

Read the extract below and then attempt the following questions.

***The Cone-Gatherers* by Robin Jenkins**

In this extract, Neil and Calum have been caught in a storm and take refuge in the summer house belonging to the Runcie-Campbell family. Calum has picked up a doll.

'Put it back, Calum,' he said.

'Would it be all right if I took it away and put a leg on it?' asked Calum eagerly. 'I would bring it back.'

'No, it would not. It would be stealing. Put it back. In any case, it's just a doll, fit for a wee
5 lassie. Put it back.'

Neil went over to attend to the fire.

'Get your jacket off, Calum,' he said, 'and hold it in front of the fire.'

As he spoke he was cautiously taking his own off. His shoulder joints were very stiff and sore.

10 'Do you know what I'm going to do?' he asked, as he was helping to take off his brother's jacket. 'I'm going to have a puff at that pipe you bought me in Lendrick.'

Calum was delighted. 'Is it a good pipe, Neil?'

'The best I ever had. It must have cost you a fortune.'

Calum laughed and shook his head. 'I'm not telling,' he said.

15 Neil was feeling in his pocket for the pipe when other noises outside were added to the drumming of the rain on the roof: a dog's bark, and voices.

As they stared towards the door, there came a scratching on it as of paws, and a whining. A minute later they heard the lady cry out 'Thank God!' and then a key rattled in the lock. The door was flung open to the accompaniment of the loudest peal of thunder since the
20 start of the storm.

From a safe distance the little dog barked at the trespassers. The lady had only a silken handkerchief over her head; her green tweed costume was black in places with damp. In the midst of the thunder she shouted: 'What is the meaning of this?' Though astonishment, and perhaps dampness, made her voice hoarse, it nevertheless was far more appalling to
25 the two men than any thunder. They could not meet the anger in her face. They gazed at her feet; her stockings were splashed with mud and her shoes had sand on them.

Neil did not know what to do or say. Every second of silent abjectness was a betrayal of himself, and especially of his brother who was innocent. All his vows of never again being ashamed of Calum were being broken. His rheumatism tortured him, as if coals from the
30 stolen fire had been pressed into his shoulders and knees; but he wished that the pain was twenty times greater to punish him as he deserved. He could not lift his head; he tried, so that he could meet the lady's gaze at least once, no matter how scornful and contemptuous it was; but he could not. A lifetime of frightened submissiveness held it down.

MARKS

Suddenly he realised that Calum was speaking.

35 'It's not Neil's fault, lady,' he was saying. 'He did it because I was cold and wet.'

'For God's sake,' muttered the lady, and Neil felt rather than saw how she recoiled from Calum, as if from something obnoxious, and took her children with her.

Questions

14. Look at lines 1—14.

     By referring to **two** examples, explain what we learn about the relationship between Calum and Neil.   4

15. Look at lines 15—20.

     By referring to **two** examples of language, explain how the writer creates tension.   4

16. Look at lines 27—37.

     By referring to **two** examples of language, explain how Neil feels at this point.   4

17. By referring to this extract and to elsewhere in the novel, show how **one** interesting character is created.   8

[Turn over

OR

Text 2 — Prose

If you choose this text you may not attempt a question on Prose in Section 2.

Read the extract below and then attempt the following questions.

The Testament of Gideon Mack **by James Robertson**

She put the car into first gear and drove off, spraying my legs with gravel. I half-thought of driving after her, but saw it was futile. She was in no mood to listen. She thought I was ill, that I had invented the whole thing about the Stone. But I knew I wasn't ill. She'd panicked because I'd said I loved her, and because she loved me too. *That* was what frightened her.

5 A crisis was upon me. I was sweating, seething with energy. If I didn't do something the energy would burst out of me and leave me wrecked on the floor. My left arm was twitching as if in contact with an electric fence. I wanted to go to the Stone, yet at the same time was afraid to go. It seemed to me that the Stone had provoked this crisis, had engineered it in some way. I paced round the manse, in and out of every room, up and
10 down the stairs. I'd just decided to get changed and head off for a long run, to try to calm down, when the bell rang again. I thought Elsie must have come back and rushed to the front door. A car had pulled up in the drive, but not Elsie's. It was Lorna Sprott.

'Gideon,' Lorna said. 'I've been at the museum. I missed the exhibition opening but I've had a good look round.' Something in my expression stopped her. 'Is this an awkward
15 moment?'

'Actually, I was about to go for a run.'

'You wouldn't like to come for a walk instead? I've got Jasper in the car. I was thinking we might go to the Black Jaws.'

I opened my mouth to make an excuse, but she didn't notice.

20 'The exhibition surprised me,' she said. 'I didn't think it would be my cup of tea at all, and I can't say I understood everything, but it was quite thought-provoking. I saw old Menteith's study and listened to you reading while I was looking down through that window. That's what put me in mind to go to the Black Jaws, the real place. I haven't been there for ages, and Jasper could do with a change from the beach.'

25 She looked pleadingly at me. How could I resist? Lorna stood on the step, inexorable and solid, and I knew I'd never get rid of her. Even if I slammed the door in her face she wouldn't leave me alone. I imagined her scraping and chapping at the windows until I let her in. 'Wait a minute,' I said, and went to get my boots and a jacket.

Perhaps I was meant to go for a walk with Lorna, to talk to her about what was going on.
30 Perhaps the Stone was wielding some strange power over events and had brought her to my door at this moment. In the minute or two it took me to get ready I made a decision. I would go with Lorna to the Black Jaws and, depending on how things went, I would swear her to secrecy, take her to Keldo Woods, and show her the Stone. I could trust her thus far, I knew. If Lorna acknowledged that the Stone existed, then I would know I was neither
35 hallucinating nor mad and I would go to Elsie and John. I would confront them with the misery and mockery of our lives and ask them to have the courage, with me, to change them. If, on the other hand, Lorna could not see the Stone, then I would have to admit that what Elsie had said was true, that I needed help.

MARKS

40 I didn't know, as I locked the manse door and got into Lorna's car, that I wouldn't be back for nearly a week. Nor could I have foreseen that I would return utterly transformed. Nor indeed, as I strapped myself in and gritted my teeth against Lorna's terrible driving, and was greeted by Jasper's happy squeals and licks from the back seat, could I have guessed that it would not be Lorna who would trigger what happened next, but her dog.

Questions

18. Look at lines 5—12.

    By referring to **two** examples of language, explain how the writer creates tension.   4

19. Look at lines 13—24.

    By referring to **one** example, explain what we learn about the character of Lorna.   2

20. Look at lines 25—38.

    Using your own words as far as possible, identify **two** reasons why Gideon decides to go to the Black Jaws with Lorna.   2

21. Look at lines 39—43.

    By referring to **two** examples of language, explain how the writer makes this moment seem dramatic.   4

22. By referring to this extract and to elsewhere in the novel, show how setting is an important feature.   8

[Turn over

OR

Text 3 — Prose

If you choose this text you may not attempt a question on Prose in Section 2.

Read the extract below and then attempt the following questions.

Kidnapped **by Robert Louis Stevenson**

In this extract, David Balfour and Alan Breck Stewart are escaping through the heather after spending some time with Cluny Macpherson.

At last, upon the other side of Loch Errocht, going over a smooth, rushy place, where the walking was easy, he could bear it no longer, and came close to me.

'David,' says he, 'this is no way for two friends to take a small accident. I have to say that I'm sorry; and so that's said. And now if you have anything, ye'd better say it.'

5 'O,' says I, 'I have nothing.'

He seemed disconcerted; at which I was meanly pleased.

'No,' said he, with rather a trembling voice, 'but when I say I was to blame?'

'Why, of course, ye were to blame,' said I, coolly; 'and you will bear me out that I have never reproached you.'

10 'Never,' says he; 'but ye ken very well that ye've done worse. Are we to part? Ye said so once before. Are ye to say it again? There's hills and heather enough between here and the two seas, David; and I will own I'm no very keen to stay where I'm no wanted.'

This pierced me like a sword, and seemed to lay bare my private disloyalty.

'Alan Breck!' I cried; and then: 'Do you think I am one to turn my back on you in your chief
15 need? You dursn't say it to my face. My whole conduct's there to give the lie to it. It's true, I fell asleep upon the muir; but that was from weariness, and you do wrong to cast it up to me —'

'Which is what I never did,' said Alan.

'But aside from that,' I continued, 'what have I done that you should even me to dogs by
20 such a supposition? I never yet failed a friend, and it's not likely I'll begin with you. There are things between us that I can never forget, even if you can.'

'I will only say this to ye, David,' said Alan, very quietly, 'that I have long been owing ye my life, and now I owe ye money. Ye should try to make that burden light for me.'

This ought to have touched me, and in a manner it did, but the wrong manner. I felt I was
25 behaving badly; and was now not only angry with Alan, but angry with myself in the bargain; and it made me the more cruel.

'You asked me to speak,' said I. 'Well, then, I will. You own yourself that you have done me a disservice; I have had to swallow an affront: I have never reproached you, I never named the thing till you did. And now you blame me,' cried I, 'because I cannae laugh and sing as
30 if I was glad to be affronted. The next thing will be that I'm to go down upon my knees and thank you for it! Ye should think more of others, Alan Breck. If ye thought more of others, ye would perhaps speak less about yourself; and when a friend that likes you very well has passed over an offence without a word, you would be blithe to let it lie, instead of making it a stick to break his back with. By your own way of it, it was you that was to blame; then
35 it shouldnae be you to seek the quarrel.'

'Aweel,' said Alan, 'say nae mair.'

And we fell back into our former silence; and came to our journey's end, and supped, and lay down to sleep, without another word.

Questions

23. Look at lines 1—9.

    By referring to **two** examples, explain how the writer makes clear the conflict between Alan and David.   **4**

24. Look at lines 13—21.

    By referring to **two** examples of language, explain how the writer reveals David's anger.   **4**

25. Look at lines 10—38.

    By referring to **two** examples, explain **two** things we learn about the character of Alan.   **4**

26. By referring to this extract and to elsewhere in the novel, show how the writer explores the theme of friendship.   **8**

[Turn over

OR

Text 4 — Prose

If you choose this text you may not attempt a question on Prose in Section 2.

Read the extract below and then attempt the following questions.

The Red Door by Iain Crichton Smith

Murdo stared at the door and as he looked at it he seemed to be drawn inside it into its deep caves with all sorts of veins and passages. It was like a magic door out of the village but at the same time it pulsed with a deep red light which made it appear alive. It was all very odd and very puzzling, to think that a red door could make such a difference to house
5   and moors and streams.

Solid and heavy he stood in front of it in his wellingtons, scratching his head. But the red door was not a mirror and he couldn't see himself in it. Rather he was sucked into it as if it were a place of heat and colour and reality. But it was different and it was his.

It was true that the villagers when they woke would see it and perhaps make fun of it, and
10   would advise him to repaint it. They might not even want him in the village if he insisted on having a red door. Still they could all have red doors if they wanted to. Or they could hunt him out of the village.

Hunt him out of the village? He paused for a moment, stunned by the thought. It had never occurred to him that he could leave the village, especially at his age, forty-six. But then
15   other people had left the village and some had prospered though it was true that many had failed. As for himself, he could work hard, he had always done so. And perhaps he had never really belonged to the village. Perhaps his belonging had been like the Hallowe'en mask. If he were a true villager would he like the door so much? Other villagers would have been angry if their door had been painted red in the night, their anger reflected in the red
20   door, but he didn't feel at all angry, in fact he felt admiration that someone should actually have thought of this, should actually have seen the possibility of a red door, in a green and black landscape.

He felt a certain childlikeness stirring within him as if he were on Christmas day stealing barefooted over the cold red linoleum to the stocking hanging at the chimney, to see if
25   Santa Claus had come in the night while he slept.

Having studied the door for a while and having had a long look round the village which was rousing itself to a new day, repetitive as all the previous ones, he turned into the house. He ate his breakfast and thinking carefully and joyously and having washed the dishes he set off to see Mary though in fact it was still early.

30   His wellingtons creaked among the sparkling frost. Its virginal new diamonds glittered around him, millions of them. Before he knocked on her door he looked at his own door from a distance. It shone bravely against the frost and the drab patches without frost or snow. There was pride and spirit about it. It had emerged out of the old and the habitual, brightly and vulnerably. It said, 'Please let me live my own life.' He knocked on the door.

MARKS

Questions

27. Look at lines 1–8.

By referring to **two** examples of language, explain how the writer suggests that the red door is unusual.

4

28. Look at lines 9–22.

Using your own words as far as possible, explain Murdo's reaction to the door. You should make **two** key points in your answer.

2

29. Look at lines 23–29.

By referring to **one** example of language, explain how the writer suggests a fresh start for Murdo.

2

30. Look at lines 30–34.

By referring to **two** examples of language, explain how the writer creates a positive mood or atmosphere.

4

31. By referring to this extract and to at least one other story by Crichton Smith, show how an important theme is explored.

8

[Turn over

OR

Text 5 — Prose

If you choose this text you may not attempt a question on Prose in Section 2.

Read the extract below and then attempt the following questions.

Away in a Manger by Anne Donovan

'Naw. Are you cauld?'

'Just ma nose.'

She covered it wi her white mitt.

A vision of warmth, a fire, a mug of hot tea rose afore Sandra's eyes.

5   'We could come back and see the lights another night.'

'Naw, Mammy, naw, we cannae go hame noo, we're nearly there, you promised . . .'

'All right, we'll go. Ah just thought you were too cauld.'

Amy had been gaun on aboot the lights for weeks; at least this would get it ower and done wi. God, she was sick of it all, specially the extra hours in the shop. Every Christmas they
10   opened longer and longer. Late-night shoppers, trippin ower wan another tae buy presents that'd be returned on Boxin Day, everybody in a bad mood, trachled wi parcels. And those bloody Christmas records playin non-stop. The extra hours meant extra money, right enough, and it wouldnae be so bad if they'd only tell you in advance, but see if that old bag of a supervisor sidled up tae her once more wi her 'Could you just do an extra couple of
15   hours tonight, Sandra?' Wanny these days she'd hit her ower the heid wi a gift-wrapped basket of Fruits of Nature toiletries.

No the night, though.

'Awful sorry, Linda. Ah'm takin Amy tae see the lights in George Square. Ma neighbour's gaun late-night shoppin so she'll bring her in tae meet me.'

20   'Amy'll love that.'

Sandra was foldin a shelf of red sweaters when Amy came intae the shop, wearin her new coat. She adored that coat, specially the hood, which had a white fur-fabric ruff round the edge. When she'd first got it she walked aboot the hoose in it wi the hood up and Sandra could hardly persuade her tae take it off at bedtime. It had been dear, too much really, but
25   Sandra always wanted Amy tae have nice things, she looked so good in them. She was a beautiful child, everybody said so; even the old bag.

'What a pretty wee girl you are. Oh, she's got gorgeous curls, Sandra.'

She pressed a coin intae Amy's haund.

'That'll buy you some sweeties, pet.'

30   'What do you say, Amy?'

'Thank you very much.'

Amy placed the coin carefully inside her mitt.

They turned the corner and the cauld evaporated. The square shimmerin wi light, brightness sharp against the gloomy street. Trees frosted wi light. Lights shaped intae
35   circles and flowers, like the plastic jewellery sets wee lassies love. Lights switchin on and off in a mad rhythm ae their ain, tryin tae look like bells ringin and snow fallin. Reindeer and Santas, holly, ivy, robins, all bleezin wi light. Amy gazed at them, eyes shinin.

MARKS

Questions

32. Look at lines 1—7.

    By referring to **one** example, explain how the writer's use of language makes it clear that Sandra is not very enthusiastic about the trip to see the lights.   2

33. Look at lines 8—16.

    By referring to **two** examples, explain how the writer's use of language makes clear Sandra's feelings about the Christmas season.   4

34. Look at lines 17—31.

    Using your own words as far as possible, explain Sandra's attitude towards her daughter, Amy, at this point in the story. You should make **two** key points in your answer.   2

35. Look at lines 32—37.

    By referring to **two** examples, explain how the writer's use of language creates a magical atmosphere.   4

36. By referring to this extract and to at least one other story by Donovan, show how important relationships are explored.   8

[Turn over

SECTION 1 — SCOTTISH TEXT — 20 marks

PART C — SCOTTISH TEXT — POETRY

Text 1 — Poetry

If you choose this text you may not attempt a question on Poetry in Section 2.

Read the extract below and then attempt the following questions.

Mrs Midas by Carol Ann Duffy

It was late September. I'd just poured a glass of wine, begun
to unwind, while the vegetables cooked. The kitchen
filled with the smell of itself, relaxed, its steamy breath
gently blanching the windows. So I opened one,
5 then with my fingers wiped the other's glass like a brow.
He was standing under the pear tree snapping a twig.

Now the garden was long and the visibility poor, the way
the dark of the ground seems to drink the light of the sky,
but that twig in his hand was gold. And then he plucked
10 a pear from a branch — we grew Fondante d'Automne —
and it sat in his palm like a light bulb. On.
I thought to myself, Is he putting fairy lights in the tree?

He came into the house. The doorknobs gleamed.
He drew the blinds. You know the mind; I thought of
15 the Field of the Cloth of Gold and of Miss Macready.
He sat in that chair like a king on a burnished throne.
The look on his face was strange, wild, vain. I said,
What in the name of God is going on? He started to laugh.

I served up the meal. For starters, corn on the cob.
20 Within seconds he was spitting out the teeth of the rich.
He toyed with his spoon, then mine, then with the knives, the forks.
He asked where was the wine. I poured with a shaking hand,
a fragrant, bone-dry white from Italy, then watched
as he picked up the glass, goblet, golden chalice, drank.

MARKS

Questions

37. Look at lines 1—6.

    By referring to **two** examples of language, explain how the writer creates a calm mood.

    4

38. Look at lines 7—12.

    By referring to **two** examples of language, explain how the writer makes it clear that the speaker feels some uncertainty.

    4

39. Look at lines 13—24.

    By referring to **two** examples of language, explain how the writer makes it clear that something dramatic is now happening.

    4

40. By referring to this extract and to at least one other poem by Duffy, show how the poet creates interesting characters.

    8

[Turn over

OR

Text 2 — Poetry

If you choose this text you may not attempt a question on Poetry in Section 2.

Read the poem below and then attempt the following questions.

Slate **by Edwin Morgan**

There is no beginning. We saw Lewis
laid down, when there was not much but thunder
and volcanic fires; watched long seas plunder
faults; laughed as Staffa cooled. Drumlins blue as
5   bruises were grated off like nutmegs; bens,
and a great glen, gave a rough back we like
to think the ages must streak, surely strike,
seldom stroke, but raised and shaken, with tens
of thousands of rains, blizzards, sea-poundings
10 shouldered off into night and memory.
Memory of men! That was to come. Great
in their empty hunger these surroundings
threw walls to the sky, the sorry glory
of a rainbow. Their heels kicked flint, chalk, slate.

MARKS

Questions

41. Look at lines 1—5.

    By referring to **two** examples, explain how the poet's use of language suggests the power and/or violence of the island's creation.   4

42. Look at lines 6—10.

    By referring to **two** examples, explain how the poet's use of language develops your understanding of the island.   4

43. Look at lines 11—14.

    By referring to **two** examples of language, explain how the poet gives a clear impression of change.   4

44. By referring to this poem and to at least one other by Morgan, show how an important theme is explored.   8

[Turn over

OR

Text 3 — Poetry

If you choose this text you may not attempt a question on Poetry in Section 2.

Read the poem below and then attempt the following questions.

Memorial *by Norman MacCaig*

Everywhere she dies. Everywhere I go she dies.
No sunrise, no city square, no lurking beautiful mountain
but has her death in it.
The silence of her dying sounds through
5 the carousel of language, it's a web
on which laughter stitches itself. How can my hand
clasp another's when between them
is that thick death, that intolerable distance?

She grieves for my grief. Dying, she tells me
10 that bird dives from the sun, that fish
leaps into it. No crocus is carved more gently
than the way her dying
shapes my mind. — But I hear, too,
the other words,
15 black words that make the sound
of soundlessness, that name the nowhere
she is continuously going into.

Ever since she died
she can't stop dying. She makes me
20 her elegy. I am a walking masterpiece,
a true fiction
of the ugliness of death.
I am her sad music.

MARKS

Questions

45. Look at the poem as a whole.

    Using your own words as far as possible, explain **two** ways in which the woman's death has affected the speaker.

    2

46. Look at lines 1—8.

    By referring to **two** examples of language, explain how the strong impact of the woman's death is made clear.

    4

47. Look at lines 9—15.

    By referring to **two** examples of language, explain how the poet suggests that the woman still seems close.

    4

48. Select an expression from lines 19—23 ('She makes me . . . sad music.'), and explain how it helps to contribute to an effective ending to the poem.

    2

49. By referring to this poem and to at least one other by MacCaig, show how the poet uses language to explore important experiences.

    8

[Turn over

OR

Text 4 — Poetry

If you choose this text you may not attempt a question on Poetry in Section 2.

Read the extract below and then attempt the following questions.

Gap Year **by Jackie Kay**

I remember your Moses basket before you were born.
I'd stare at the fleecy white sheet for days, weeks,
willing you to arrive, hardly able to believe
I would ever have a real baby to put in the basket.

5 I'd feel the mound of my tight tub of a stomach,
and you moving there, foot against my heart,
elbow in my ribcage, turning, burping, awake, asleep.
One time I imagined I felt you laugh.

I'd play you Handel's *Water Music* or Emma Kirkby
10 singing Pergolesi. I'd talk to you, my close stranger,
call you Tumshie, ask when you were coming to meet me.
You arrived late, the very hot summer of eighty-eight.

You had passed the due date string of eights,
and were pulled out with forceps, blue, floury,
15 on the fourteenth of August on Sunday afternoon.
I took you home on Monday and lay you in your basket.

Now, I peek in your room and stare at your bed
hardly able to imagine you back in there sleeping,
Your handsome face — soft, open. Now you are eighteen,
20 six foot two, away, away in Costa Rica, Peru, Bolivia.

I follow your trails on my *Times Atlas*:
from the Caribbean side of Costa Rica to the Pacific,
the baby turtles to the massive leatherbacks.
Then on to Lima, to Cuzco. Your grandfather

25 rings: 'Have you considered altitude sickness,
Christ, he's sixteen thousand feet above sea level.'
Then to the lost city of the Incas, Machu Picchu,
Where you take a photograph of yourself with the statue

of the original Tupac. You are wearing a Peruvian hat.
30 Yesterday in Puno before catching the bus for Copacabana,
you suddenly appear on a webcam and blow me a kiss,
you have a new haircut; your face is grainy, blurry.

MARKS

Questions

50. Look at lines 1—4.

    By referring to **one** example of language, explain how the poet creates a mood of excitement.

    2

51. Look at lines 5—12.

    By referring to **two** examples of language, explain how the poet suggests a strong bond between mother and baby.

    4

52. Look at lines 17—32.

    (a) By referring to **two** examples of language, explain how the poet makes clear the mother's feelings about her son being away.

    4

    (b) By referring to **one** example of language, explain how the grandfather reveals a different point of view.

    2

53. By referring to this extract and to at least one other poem by Kay, show how setting is an important feature.

    8

[END OF SECTION 1]

[Turn over

SECTION 2 — CRITICAL ESSAY — 20 marks

Attempt ONE question from the following genres — Drama, Prose, Poetry, Film and Television Drama, or Language.

Your answer must be on a different genre from that chosen in Section 1.

You should spend approximately 45 minutes on this Section.

DRAMA

> *Answers to questions in this part should refer to the text and to such relevant features as characterisation, key scene(s), structure, climax, theme, plot, conflict, setting . . .*

1. Choose a play in which the writer creates an interesting character.

    By referring to appropriate techniques, explain how the writer makes this character interesting.

2. Choose a play which explores an important theme.

    By referring to appropriate techniques, explain how this theme is explored.

PROSE

> *Answers to questions in this part should refer to the text and to such relevant features as characterisation, setting, language, key incident(s), climax, turning point, plot, structure, narrative technique, theme, ideas, description . . .*

3. Choose a novel **or** short story **or** a work of non-fiction which deals with a significant event or experience or issue.

    Give a brief account of the significant event or experience or issue. By referring to appropriate techniques, explain how it is important to the text as a whole.

4. Choose a novel **or** short story in which there is a character you feel strongly about.

    By referring to appropriate techniques, explain how the author creates this reaction in you.

POETRY

Answers to questions in this part should refer to the text and to such relevant features as word choice, tone, imagery, structure, content, rhythm, rhyme, theme, sound, ideas . . .

5. Choose a poem which explores an aspect of human experience.

    By referring to poetic techniques, explain how this aspect of human experience is explored.

6. Choose a poem which makes effective use of setting.

    By referring to poetic techniques, explain how the setting adds to your appreciation of the poem as a whole.

FILM AND TELEVISION DRAMA

Answers to questions in this part should refer to the text and to such relevant features as use of camera, key sequence, characterisation, mise-en-scène, editing, setting, music/sound, special effects, plot, dialogue . . .

7. Choose a film **or** TV drama* which has a memorable character.

    By referring to appropriate techniques, explain how the director makes the character memorable throughout the film or TV drama.

8. Choose a scene or sequence from a film **or** TV drama* in which setting is an important feature.

    By referring to appropriate techniques, explain how the director presents the setting in this scene or sequence.

* 'TV drama' includes a single play, a series or a serial.

[Turn over

LANGUAGE

Answers to questions in this part should refer to the text and to such relevant features as register, accent, dialect, slang, jargon, vocabulary, tone, abbreviation . . .

9.   Choose an example of language which aims to persuade you to agree with a particular point of view, **or** to buy a product, **or** to influence your behaviour.

     By referring to specific examples, explain how persuasive language is used effectively.

10. Choose an example of language used by a group of people from the same place, **or** with the same job, **or** of the same age, **or** who have shared similar experiences.

     By referring to specific examples, explain the features of this language.

[END OF SECTION 2]

[END OF QUESTION PAPER]

NATIONAL 5

2019

National Qualifications 2016

X724/75/11

English
Reading for Understanding, Analysis and Evaluation

THURSDAY, 5 MAY

1:00 PM – 2:00 PM

Total marks — 30

Attempt ALL questions.

Write your answers clearly in the answer booklet provided. In the answer booklet you must clearly identify the question number you are attempting.

Use **blue** or **black** ink.

Before leaving the examination room you must give your answer booklet to the Invigilator; if you do not, you may lose all the marks for this paper.

Can Idina Menzel ever Let It Go?

When the organisers of the 2015 Super Bowl were looking for someone to follow in the footsteps of Diana Ross and Whitney Houston and belt out *The Star-Spangled Banner* in front of a global audience of 160 million, it's not hard to see why they chose Idina Menzel.

5   As the voice of Elsa the ice queen in *Frozen*, the most successful animated film of all time, who sang its ubiquitous Oscar-winning *Let It Go* (more than three million copies sold in America alone), she has a more than passing acquaintance with anthems.

The stratospheric success of *Frozen* — with takings of more than £800 million, it's No 5 in the all-time list of highest-grossing films — has elevated her into a new league.

Now she releases hit Christmas albums, has Broadway shows written for her, tours the
10   world's mega-domes and is having a TV sitcom developed.

Frozen isn't going away, either. She's spoken in the past about the much-mooted sequel but she has clearly been reprimanded by the Disney suits: "Apparently I spoke out of turn. I just assumed that because it was so successful there'd be a sequel, but Disney doesn't have sequels, so it would be a first if there was one."

15   How about the *Frozen* stage show, also much mooted? "I think they're working on that but the Disney people keep things close to their chests." If it happens, would she like to be in it? "Sure, I'd love to. But musicals take years and I'd have to play Elsa's mother, probably!"

What's definitely happening is a six-minute short, *Frozen Fever*, in which Elsa's powers threaten to scupper the birthday of her sister, Anna. "It's fun, really clever," Menzel says.
20   "There's a new song. It's pretty much a group number though." She sounds slightly disappointed.

Frozen Fever did delight both fans and Disney — it was shown in cinemas before Disney's live-action *Cinderella*, which doubtless enjoyed a mighty bump as a result. The studio may be tight-lipped about *Frozen* sequels, but they're certainly happy to milk the
25   commercial opportunities of their icy behemoth.

Whether there is a *Frozen 2* or not, Menzel is now a big star, there to be shot at. When she performed *Let It Go* in Times Square in New York on New Year's Eve she was criticised for failing to hit a high note (to be fair, she was singing in sub-zero temperatures). And though her powerful, stately turn at the Super Bowl received strong reviews, there were
30   still some who noticed the odd flat note.

The unnerving proximity of several dozen hulking American footballers may have had something to do with that. Talking about the time that she sang at the All-Star baseball game, Menzel says: "One thing I underestimated is what a strong presence these athletes have when they're standing on the line right in front of you. They're huge, standing
35   there, and you're this one woman, singing on her own. You forget about the world and the rest of the stadium because they're so . . . daunting."

One woman opposite a squad of men: it's a pertinent image given her associations with *Frozen*, a film that has regularly been touted as a feminist breakthrough. The first Disney animation to be directed (well, co-directed) by a woman, Jennifer Lee, it's quietly
40   revolutionary because, as Menzel says, "the purest love that's being celebrated is between two sisters and not because some Prince Charming is saving the day".

Yes, the two heroines are still doe-eyed and partial to shiny dresses, but their relationship is subtle: Elsa, the conflicted snow sorceress struggling to control her powers; Anna, the devoted younger sister whom she keeps at a distance for fear of turning her into a
45   popsicle. With her grandiose sulks, Elsa has been described as Disney's first emo princess. "She's definitely complicated," Menzel says. "I think that's why it's a successful film, because both women are not stereotypes."

There are parallels with Menzel's own life: she and her younger sister, Cara, had their fair share of "Do you wanna build a snowman?" moments. "She would probably tell you she
50   looks up to me, a lot," Menzel says, rather wincingly.

When *Let It Go* was nominated for Best Song at the Oscars a year ago, it was Cara whom Menzel took as her date. "I didn't think about it — she was the first person I thought of — and then I realised how perfect it was," she says. Sisters representing a film about sisters.

55   *Let It Go* won the Oscar for its writers, but that was rather overshadowed by the moment of weirdness earlier in the evening when, introducing Menzel's performance of the song, John Travolta inexplicably referred to her as "Adele Dazeem".

She nevertheless recognises that Travolta's slip was "one of the greatest mistakes ever — it helped my career, that's for sure." It's one of several references Menzel makes
60   to her career: her conversation is a mix of Broadway-speak ("I try to sing from the heart") and battle-hardened ambition.

She is certainly aware of the value of appearing in "several zeitgeist-y things across different generations: from *Rent* to *Wicked*, *Glee* to *Frozen*". There's a 'through line' between those four, she thinks: they all resonate with young people and "people who are
65   trying to find themselves. I'm proud of that. I'm not sure why that's become the pattern for me — maybe it's because I have as much to learn myself".

Our time is almost up. I'm allowed to ask one more (burning) question. Does she have her own Elsa dress, the must-have wardrobe item for girls across the western world? "No I do not!" she laughs.

70   So she doesn't ever have the urge to indulge her inner ice queen and don the full regalia? "Nah, I don't look that good as a blonde. The waistline, though — that would be fun." Part of me suspects that she'd also quite enjoy ruling over her own wintry kingdom.

Ed Potton, in "The Times"

MARKS

Total marks — 30

Attempt ALL Questions

1. Look at lines 1—6, and then explain **in your own words** why the organisers of the Super Bowl chose Idina Menzel to perform there.

   2

2. Look at lines 7—8, and then, by referring to **one** example, explain fully how the writer's use of language makes it clear that Frozen is successful.

   2

3. Look at lines 11—25, and then identify, **using your own words** as far as possible, **five** things we learn here about the Disney organisation.

   5

4. Look at lines 26—36, and then explain fully how the writer's use of language makes it clear that coping with performing under these circumstances is not easy. You should refer to **two** examples in your answer.

   4

5. By referring to the sentence in lines 37—38, explain how it helps to provide a link between the writer's ideas at this point in the passage.

   2

6. Look at lines 42—47, and then explain fully how **two** examples of the writer's **word choice** make it clear that Elsa is not just "doe-eyed and partial to shiny dresses".

   4

7. Look at lines 51—61, and then explain fully **in your own words** as far as possible why the Oscar evening was so memorable or such a success for Idina Menzel.

   2

8. Look at lines 62—69, by referring to **two** examples, explain fully how the writer makes effective use of contrast in these paragraphs. You could refer to sentence structure, tone or word choice.

   4

9. Throughout the passage, we are given information and clues about Idina Menzel's personality.

   Using your own words as far as possible, identify **five** things that we learn about her personality from the passage.

   5

[END OF QUESTION PAPER]

Page five

OPEN OUT FOR QUESTIONS

DO NOT WRITE ON THIS PAGE

[BLANK PAGE]

DO NOT WRITE ON THIS PAGE

National Qualifications 2019

X824/75/12

English
Critical Reading

THURSDAY, 9 MAY

10:30 AM — 12:00 NOON

Total marks — 40

SECTION 1 — Scottish Text — 20 marks

Read an extract from a Scottish text you have previously studied.

Choose ONE text from either

Part A — Drama   Pages 2–7

or

Part B — Prose   Pages 8–17

or

Part C — Poetry   Pages 18–25

Attempt ALL the questions for your chosen text.

SECTION 2 — Critical Essay — 20 marks

Attempt ONE question from the following genres — Drama, Prose, Poetry, Film and Television Drama, or Language.

Your answer must be on a different genre from that chosen in Section 1.

You should spend approximately 45 minutes on each section.

Write your answers clearly in the answer booklet provided. In the answer booklet you must clearly identify the question number you are attempting.

Use **blue** or **black** ink.

Before leaving the examination room you must give your answer booklet to the Invigilator; if you do not, you may lose all the marks for this paper.

SECTION 1 — SCOTTISH TEXT — 20 marks

PART A — SCOTTISH TEXT — DRAMA

Text 1 — Drama

If you choose this text you may not attempt a question on Drama in Section 2.

Read the extract below and then attempt the following questions.

Bold Girls by Rona Munro

Extract from Scene Four (Marie and Deirdre are in Marie's house . . .)

MARIE: It wasn't that I lied. I just didn't tell all the truth that was in me. Sure, what good would telling that kind of truth do you? You'd be crazy to talk about it wouldn't you? What man would listen to that? If he heard you he'd have to change. Maybe he'd sooner leave. I didn't want him to leave. I loved him. I can't throw that away
5   even now. I loved him. You see I'm just a mug, Deirdre. Cassie was right. I knew who you were the first time I saw you. I knew. (*Pause*) What age are you?

DEIRDRE: I'm sixteen.

MARIE: (*sucking in her breath*) I was married sixteen years.

DEIRDRE: I know.

10 *There is a pause*

MARIE: Sometimes — sometimes when he came home he'd cry, from tiredness, because his heart was sick in him. He'd cry and I'd comfort him.

Deirdre pushes at the money on the table for a minute

DEIRDRE: I'll get the other fiver for you.

15 MARIE: It doesn't matter.

DEIRDRE: It's your money.

MARIE: It's Cassie's now. It'll go back to her. She needs it to dream with. (*She shakes her head*) She'll not use it for much else. You're shivering.

DEIRDRE: I've cold blood. That's what they say . . . I'm away now. (*She gets up*)

20 MARIE: You can't go out like that.

Deirdre pulls the blanket round her; she looks at Marie

MARIE: Your daddy . . . Your daddy was a man, like any other. If he knew you were alive he never told me. And he's dead now . . . You've got his eyes.

They look at each other for a minute

25 *Deirdre nods*

DEIRDRE: I'll be away up the road then.

MARIE: Not at this hour, it's nearly morning. I'll get the breakfast started. Come on you'll be hungry soon. (*She moves back to the kitchen and starts getting out food*) You can give me a hand if you like.

30 *Deirdre hesitates, then goes to join her*

MARKS

MARIE: (*Handing her a loaf*) Slice the top crust off that bread but keep it.

DEIRDRE: What for?

MARIE: For the birds. Did you ever feed the birds, Deirdre?

DEIRDRE: No.

35 MARIE: I like the common wee birds, the pigeons and the starlings and the sparrows, it's easy enough to build a great wee nest when you've a whole forest to fly in, but you'd need to be something special to build one round the Falls. Someone should feed them. (*Pause*) You make crumbs of that. I'll put the kettle on.

Lights fade to Black-out

Questions

1. Using your own words as far as possible, summarise what happens in this extract.

   You should make **four** key points.   4

2. Look at lines 1—6.

   By referring to **two** examples of language, explain how the playwright reveals Marie's thoughts and/or feelings in these lines.   4

3. Look at lines 7—39.

   By referring to **one** example of speech and **one** stage direction, explain how Marie shows Deirdre kindness.   4

4. By referring to this extract and to elsewhere in the play, show how the playwright explores family relationships.   8

[Turn over

OR

Text 2 — Drama

If you choose this text you may not attempt a question on Drama in Section 2.

Read the extract below and then attempt the following questions.

Sailmaker **by Alan Spence**

(DAVIE is sitting in chair, reading newspaper. ALEC enters, singing.)

	ALEC:	*(Sings)*
		Give me oil in my lamp keep me burning
		Give me oil in my lamp I pray
5		Halleluja!
		Give me oil in my lamp keep me burning
		Keep me burning till the break of day
	DAVIE:	Right wee religious fanatic these days eh? What is it the night then, the bandy hope?
10	ALEC:	Christian Endeavour. Band a Hope's on Thursday.
	DAVIE:	Ah thought Christian Endeavour was last night?
	ALEC:	That was just the Juniors. Tonight's the real one.
	DAVIE:	Are ye no too young?
	ALEC:	The minister says ah can come.
15	DAVIE:	Is that because ye were top in the bible exam?
	ALEC:	Top equal. Ah don't know if that's why. He just said ah could come.
	DAVIE:	Ach well, keeps ye aff the streets!
	ALEC:	Ah'll be the youngest there.
	DAVIE:	Mind yer heid in the door. Ye'll get stuck!
20	ALEC:	*(Peering at himself in shaving mirror)* This wee mirror ae yours is really stupid!
	DAVIE:	What's up wi it?
	ALEC:	Look at it! There's a big crack doon the middle. The two halfs don't sit right — aw squinty.
	DAVIE:	Does me fine for shavin.
25	ALEC:	Canny get a good look at yerself. It's dead annoyin.
	DAVIE:	Ach away ye go!
	ALEC:	Seen ma bible?
	DAVIE:	Try lookin where ye left it. *(ALEC looks around)* What's that under thae papers?
	ALEC:	Where?

Page four

MARKS

30   DAVIE: There. (*Picks up book*) Naw. It's yer prize fae the Sunday School. (*Reads*) The Life of David Livingstone. Good book that. Ah read it when ah was a boy, when ah was in the Boy's Brigade. Funny, it made me want to be a missionary maself. Great White Doctor an that. Off tae darkest Africa.

     ALEC: So what happened?

35   DAVIE: Och, ye know. Just . . . drifted away fae it. Ended up in darkest Govan instead! (*Reads label in book*) Glasgow City Mission. First Prize (Equal). Bible knowledge.

     ALEC: The questions were a skoosh. Who carried Christ's cross on the way to Calvary? And stuff fae the Catechism. Into what estate did the fall bring mankind? Dead easy. Just a matter of rememberin.

40   DAVIE: Ach aye, ye take yer brains fae yer mother son. She was clever ye know. Just wurnae the same opportunities when we were young. You stick in son. Get yerself a good education. Get a decent job. Collar and tie. Never have tae take yer jacket off.

     (*Reads*) First Prize.

45   Ah was in the B.B. for a long time ye know.

     Sure and Stedfast! (*Sings*)

     Will your anchor hold

     In the storms of life

     When the clouds unfold

50   Their wings of strife

Questions

5.   Look at lines 1—16.

   By referring to **two** examples, explain how Alec's enthusiasm for church activities is made clear.   4

6.   Look at lines 17—29.

   By referring to **two** examples, explain how Alec and Davie's relationship is presented at this point in the play.   4

7.   Look at lines 30—50.

   By referring to **two** examples, explain what is revealed about Davie's character.   4

8.   By referring to this extract and to elsewhere in the play, show how the issue of social class is an important feature of the play.   8

[Turn over

OR

Text 3 — Drama

If you choose this text you may not attempt a question on Drama in Section 2.

Read the extract below and then attempt the following questions.

Tally's Blood **by Ann Marie di Mambro**

MASSIMO:	Italy coming into the war. It's looking bad, Rosie.
ROSINELLA:	What's that got to do with us?
MASSIMO:	We're Italian, aren't we?
ROSINELLA:	So what? We just live here. We're just ordinary working people.
5 MASSIMO:	But if Italy's at war with this country —
ROSINELLA:	(*Interrupting*) Italians are good for this country. Who else is prepared to work till eleven o'clock every night, eh? You tell me that. And we work for ourselves, it's no as if we take any jobs away from any Scotch people. We stick together, pay our own way, stick to the laws. What more do they want?

10 *Hughie, arms outstretched, making aeroplane noises, comes 'flying' across the stage, making shooting noises — 'pee-aiow, pee-aiow'.*

Lucia saunters in: looks at him disdainfully: he circles her, still an aeroplane.

HUGHIE:	Pee-aiow, pee-aiow! Pee-aiow, pee-aiow!

Lucia continues to look at him with contempt which begins to fade as she becomes
15 *uncomfortable.*

Freeze on Hughie and Lucia.

Pick up on Massimo and Rosinella.

MASSIMO:	Maybe we should go back to Italy, Rosie. While we still can.
ROSINELLA 20	No. We've worked hard for everything we've got. We're no going to throw it all away.

Freeze on Massimo and Rosinella: pick up on Hughie and Lucia: he continues to circle her, shooting sounds getting louder.

HUGHIE:	Pee-aiow, pee-aiow! Pee-aiow, pee-aiow! Pee-aiow, pee-aiow!

Lucia cowering, threatened by it.

25 *Freeze on Hughie and Lucia: pick up on Massimo and Rosinella.*

MASSIMO:	I'm frightened, Rosie.
ROSINELLA:	What for? Everybody likes you.

Freeze on Massimo and Rosinella: pick up on Lucia and Hughie.

He is still making shooting noises, she is still cowering: it dawns on her it is a game, she
30 *comes out of it: kicks Hughie on the shin.*

MARKS

LUCIA: Beat it, Hughie Devlin!

Hughie rubs his shin.

HUGHIE: I don't like this game.

LUCIA: And I don't like it either.

35 *She struts off.*

Pick up on Massimo.

MASSIMO: I've lived here since I was a wee boy. I went to school here, my brother was born here, my mammy's buried here. I always thought I was lucky. I had two countries. Now I feel I've got nowhere.

Questions

9. Look at lines 6—9.

Using your own words as far as possible, summarise the reasons that Rosinella gives to support her statement that 'Italians are good for this country.'

You should make **two** key points.   2

10. Look at lines 18—27.

Using your own words as far as possible, summarise the disagreement(s) between Massimo and Rosinella.

You should make **two** key points.   2

11. Look at lines 37—39.

By referring to **two** examples of language, explain how the playwright reveals Massimo's thoughts and/or feelings.   4

12. By referring to **two** examples from anywhere in the extract, explain why the action and/or speech involving Lucia and Hughie is important.   4

13. By referring to this extract and to elsewhere in the play, show how the theme of war is explored.   8

[Turn over

SECTION 1 — SCOTTISH TEXT — 20 marks

PART B — SCOTTISH TEXT — PROSE

Text 1 — Prose

If you choose this text you may not attempt a question on Prose in Section 2.

Read the extract below and then attempt the following questions.

The Cone-Gatherers by Robin Jenkins

Delighted to be out of this bondage of talk, Calum set his bag of cones firmly round his shoulders, and with consummate confidence and grace began the descent through the inner night of the great tree. Not once, all the long way down, was he at a loss. He seemed to find holds by instinct, and patiently guided his brother's feet on to them. Alone, Neil
5 would have been in trouble; he was as dependent on his brother as if he was blind; and Calum made no attempt to make his superiority as climber compensate for his inferiority as talker. Every time he caught his brother's foot and set it on a safe branch it was an act of love. Once, when Neil slid down quicker than he meant and stamped on Calum's fingers, the latter uttered no complaint but smiled in the dark and sucked the bruise.

10 It was different as soon as they were on the ground. Neil immediately strode out, and Calum, hurrying to keep close behind, often stumbled. Gone were the balance and sureness he had shown in the tree. If there was a hollow or a stone or a stick, he would trip over it. He never grumbled at such mishaps, but scrambled up at once, anxious only not to be a hindrance to his brother.

15 When they reached the beginning of the ride that divided a cluster of Norway spruces, Neil threw over his shoulder the usual warning: to leave the snares alone, whether there were rabbits in them half throttled or hungry or frantic; and Calum gave the usual sad guilty promise.

During their very first day in the wood they had got into trouble with the gamekeeper.
20 Calum had released two rabbits from snares. Neil had been angry and had prophesied trouble. It had come next evening when Duror, the big keeper, had been waiting for them outside their hut. His rage had been quiet but intimidating. Neil had said little in reply, but had faced up to the gun raised once or twice to emphasise threats. Calum, demoralised as always by hatred, had cowered against the hut, hiding his face.

25 Duror had sworn that he would seize the first chance to hound them out of the wood; they were in it, he said, sore against his wish. Neil therefore had made Calum swear by an oath which he didn't understand but which to Neil was the most sacred on earth: by their dead mother, he had to swear never again to interfere with the snares. He could not remember his mother, who had died soon after he was born.

30 Now this evening, as he trotted down the ride, he prayed by a bright star above that there would be no rabbits squealing in pain. If there were, he could not help them; he would have to rush past, tears in his eyes, fingers in his ears.

MARKS

Questions

14. Look at lines 1—7 ('Delighted to be . . . as talker').

    By referring to **two** examples of language, explain how the writer shows Calum's skill while he is in the trees.   4

15. Look at lines 10—14.

    By referring to **one** example of language, explain how the writer shows Calum's lack of skill when he is 'on the ground'.   2

16. Look at lines 21—24 ('It had come . . . his face').

    By referring to **one** example of language for each character, explain how each of the men reacts to the conflict.

    (a) Duror   2

    (b) Neil   2

    (c) Calum   2

17. By referring to this extract and to elsewhere in the novel, show how the relationship between Neil and Calum is presented.   8

[Turn over

OR

Text 2 — Prose

If you choose this text you may not attempt a question on Prose in Section 2.

Read the extract below and then attempt the following questions.

The Testament of Gideon Mack by James Robertson

At tea-time one evening in the spring of 1966, he made an announcement.

'I have ordered a television set,' he said.

We stared at him, my mother with incomprehension and I with a tiny, thrilling hope that this might not be a perverse attempt at a joke. Almost all my school mates had television,
5   or their neighbours had, but there had never been any question of it being allowed in the manse. It was like alcohol in that respect. My father's opinion had always been that television was a distillation of all the vices he most detested. Furthermore, John Logie Baird notwithstanding, he associated it with America, in his mind the wellspring of those selfsame vices. And now here he was, telling us he intended to bring this monster into the
10 manse.

'A television set,' was all my mother said. I, for fear of betraying secret desires, didn't dare speak.

'We must move with the times,' my father said implausibly. 'I would like to see the news rather than just listen to it. There are, I believe, some good educational programmes which
15 you may enjoy, Gideon. It will be useful for other things too, major sporting events and the like.'

'I see,' said my mother, although she didn't, having even less interest in football than I had. But this was the end of April. I knew the World Cup finals were to take place in England in July: clearly my father could not resist the thought of watching Pele and the other
20 Brazilians, the Italians, the Russians and, most of all, the Portuguese, with their star player Eusebio. To do this, he required a television. It was despised and unwanted but necessary. A necessary evil, in fact.

'The licence fee and rental cost are not unreasonable,' he went on. 'We will take it on trial for three months, and if I see no harm in it, it can remain.'

25 Thus my father admitted a television — black and white, still, in 1966 — into the back parlour. It came with an internal aerial that you had to move around the room to get the best picture. Although the idea had been entirely his, my father treated the television from the day of its arrival with a kind of suppressed horror: it wasn't actually part of the contract with Radio Rentals that if its output proved corrosive to the morals of his wife and
30 son it would be removed at once, but it might as well have been. He glowered at the box in the parlour as if it were a guest of extremely doubtful character and it was only a matter of time before it did something outrageously offensive. And on the second-last day of July it did: it showed England winning the World Cup. Still, it had also allowed him to watch international football at the highest level. Furthermore, he had let the beast in, and it
35 would be an admission of error if he had to put it out again. The television remained, and gradually the rules that governed what was watched, and when, were relaxed.

Two things, however, were beyond the pale. One was watching 'American trash': shows like *The Munsters*, *Mr Ed* and *Bewitched*, none of which my father knew anything about, but all of which I homed in on rapidly, picking up information from school and then watching
40 surreptitiously whenever I could. The other was switching on the set on a Sunday.

MARKS

Questions

18. Look at lines 3—10.

By referring to **two** examples of language, explain how the writer suggests the family's surprise.

4

19. Look at lines 13—16.

Using your own words as far as possible, identify **two** reasons Gideon's father gives for wanting a television.

2

20. Look at lines 25—36.

By referring to **two** examples of language, explain how the writer reveals the father's attitude to the television.

4

21. Look at lines 37—40.

Using your own words as far as possible, identify the **two** rules about the television which had to be followed.

2

22. By referring to this extract and to elsewhere in the novel, show how Robertson explores family relationships.

8

[Turn over

OR

Text 3 — Prose

If you choose this text you may not attempt a question on Prose in Section 2.

Read the extract below and then attempt the following questions.

The Strange Case of Dr Jekyll and Mr Hyde by Robert Louis Stevenson

From that time forward, Mr Utterson began to haunt the door in the bystreet of shops. In the morning before office hours, at noon when business was plenty and time scarce, at night under the face of the fogged city moon, by all lights and at all hours of solitude or concourse, the lawyer was to be found on his chosen post.

5   'If he be Mr Hyde,' he had thought, 'I shall be Mr Seek.'

And at last his patience was rewarded. It was a fine dry night; frost in the air; the streets as clean as a ballroom floor; the lamps, unshaken by any wind, drawing a regular pattern of light and shadow. By ten o'clock, when the shops were closed, the bystreet was very solitary and, in spite of the low growl of London from all round, very silent. Small sounds
10 carried far; domestic sounds out of the houses were clearly audible on either side of the roadway; and the rumour of the approach of any passenger preceded him by a long time. Mr Utterson had been some minutes at his post, when he was aware of an odd, light footstep drawing near. In the course of his nightly patrols, he had long grown accustomed to the quaint effect with which the footfalls of a single person, while he is still a great way
15 off, suddenly spring out distinct from the vast hum and clatter of the city. Yet his attention had never before been so sharply and decisively arrested; and it was with a strong, superstitious prevision of success that he withdrew into the entry of the court.

The steps drew swiftly nearer, and swelled out suddenly louder as they turned the end of the street. The lawyer, looking forth from the entry, could soon see what manner of man
20 he had to deal with. He was small and very plainly dressed, and the look of him, even at that distance, went somehow strongly against the watcher's inclination. But he made straight for the door, crossing the roadway to save time; and as he came, he drew a key from his pocket like one approaching home.

Mr Utterson stepped out and touched him on the shoulder as he passed. 'Mr Hyde, I think?'

25 Mr Hyde shrank back with a hissing intake of the breath. But his fear was only momentary; and though he did not look the lawyer in the face, he answered coolly enough: 'That is my name. What do you want?'

'I see you are going in,' returned the lawyer. 'I am an old friend of Dr Jekyll's — Mr Utterson of Gaunt Street — you must have heard my name; and meeting you so
30 conveniently, I thought you might admit me.'

'You will not find Dr Jekyll; he is from home,' replied Mr Hyde, blowing in the key. And then suddenly, but still without looking up, 'How did you know me?' he asked.

'On your side,' said Mr Utterson, 'will you do me a favour?'

'With pleasure,' replied the other. 'What shall it be?'

35 'Will you let me see your face?' asked the lawyer.

Mr Hyde appeared to hesitate, and then, as if upon some sudden reflection, fronted about with an air of defiance; and the pair stared at each other pretty fixedly for a few seconds. 'Now I shall know you again,' said Mr Utterson. 'It may be useful.'

MARKS

Questions

23. Look at lines 1—5.

    By referring to **two** examples of language, explain how the writer makes it clear that Mr Utterson is determined to find Mr Hyde.   4

24. Look at lines 6—17.

    By referring to **two** examples of language, explain how the writer creates suspense and/or tension.   4

25. Look at lines 25—38.

    By referring to **two** examples, explain what impression is given of the character of Mr Hyde.   4

26. By referring to this extract and to elsewhere in the novel, show how Stevenson explores the theme of secrets.   8

[Turn over

OR

Text 4 — Prose

If you choose this text you may not attempt a question on Prose in Section 2.

Read the extract below and then attempt the following questions.

Mother and Son by Iain Crichton Smith

The clock struck five wheezingly and, at the first chime, the woman woke up. She started as she saw the figure crouched over the fire and then subsided: 'It's only you.' There was relief in the voice, but there was a curious hint of contempt or acceptance. He still sat staring into the fire and answered dully: 'Yes, it's only me!' He couldn't be said to speak the
5 words: they fell away from him as sometimes happens when one is in a deep reverie where every question is met by its answer almost instinctively.

'Well, what's the matter with you!' she snapped pettishly, 'sitting there moping with the tea to be made. I sometimes don't know why we christened you John' — with a sigh. 'My father was never like you. He was a man who knew his business.'

10 'All right, *all* right,' he said despairingly. 'Can't you get a new record for your gramophone. I've heard all that before,' as if he were conscious of the inadequacy of this familiar retort — he added: 'hundreds of times.' But she wasn't to be stopped.

'I can't understand what has come over you lately. You keep mooning about the house, pacing up and down with your hands in your pockets. Do you know what's going to happen
15 to you, you'll be taken to the asylum. That's where you'll go. Your father's people had something wrong with their heads, it was in your family but not in ours.' (She had always looked upon him as her husband's son, not as her own: and all his faults she attributed to hereditary weaknesses on his father's side.)

He pottered about, putting water in the kettle, waiting desperately for the sibilant noise to
20 stop. But no, it took a long time to stop. He moved about inside this sea of sound trying to keep detached, trying to force himself from listening. Sometimes, at rarer and rarer intervals, he could halt and watch her out of a clear, cold mind as if she didn't matter, as if her chatter which eddied round and round, then burst venomously towards him, had no meaning for him, could not touch him. At these times her little bitter barbs passed over
25 him or through him to come out on the other side. Most often however they stung him and stood quivering in his flesh, and he would say something angrily with the reflex of the wound. But she always cornered him. She had so much patience, and then again she enjoyed pricking him with her subtle arrows. He had now become so sensitive that he usually read some devilish meaning into her smallest utterance.

30 'Have you stacked all the sheaves now?' she was asking. He swung round on his eddying island as if he had seen that the seas were relenting, drawing back. At such moments he became deferential.

MARKS

Questions

27. Look at lines 1—6.

By referring to **two** examples of language, explain how the writer makes clear two **different** attitudes the mother has towards her son.   4

28. Look at lines 7—18.

By referring to **two** examples of language, explain how conflict between the mother and son is made clear.   4

29. Look at lines 19—32.

By referring to **two** examples of language, explain how the writer makes clear the son's reaction to the conflict with his mother.   4

30. By referring to this extract and to at least one other story by Crichton Smith, show how he presents characters who are lonely **and/or** isolated.   8

[Turn over

OR

Text 5 — Prose

If you choose this text you may not attempt a question on Prose in Section 2.

Read the extract below and then attempt the following questions.

Hieroglyphics **by Anne Donovan**

In this extract Mary is "doing a timed composition" as instructed by her teacher.

So ah startit tae write aboot ma journey tae the next world and the hings ah wid take wi me, aw in wee pictures. Ah drew me and ma mammy (ma da might as well be in the next world fur aw ah see of him) and ma sisters, Catherine an Elizabeth, in a wee boat fur ah hud some idea that ah wanted ma journey tae be ower the watter. And we took nice stuff
5 tae eat, big plates a mince an tatties (ah know ye couldnae really keep them hot but it kinda makes sense the way the Egyptians dae it) and ice cream fae the café an bottles a ginger and sweeties and that.

Ah spent a long time thinkin oot whit else ah wanted tae take, fur a loaty the hings we huv in this world might no be oany use tae us in the next. After aw, whit use are CDs if there's
10 nae electricity? So ah decided tae gie each ae us three hings tae take in the boat fur ye widnae want that much stuff that the boat wid sink, an oanyway three is wanny they numbers that's gey important in stories. Who ever heardy emdy gettin five wishes aff their fairy godmother or the two blind mice or seventeen wee pigs?

Elizabeth's three hings were easy fur she's only four an she aye cairries a bitty auld blanket
15 roond wi her, and she'll no go oanywhere wioot her teddy or her Sindy doll. Catherine's eight but she would need tae take her teddy too and her new blue jumper wi a picture of a wee lamb on it an her deelie-boablers; ye know they hings ye pit roond yer heid like an Alice band but they've got wee antennas stickin oot fae them an they make ye look lik sumpn fae ooter space. Ah know these kindy hings go in and ooty fashion and two weeks
20 fae noo she'll feel like a real chookie when she minds she wanted tae go tae mass in them, but at the moment she'd want tae take them. And ah'd take some paper and the black pen fur daein ma hieroglyphics, and ma picture ae a wee spaniel pup that ah cut oot of a magazine and keep on the wall by ma bed, fur we couldnae huv a real dug doon ma bit.

But whit would ma mammy take wi her? Aw ae a sudden it came tae me that ah didnae
25 know whit ma mammy wid take on her journey tae the next world, it wud need tae be sumpn private and jist fur her, and mammys don't tell ye these things fur they're too busy workin and bringin ye up tae huv a loaty time fur theirsels. And then auld Kelly told us tae finish off, it wis time, so ah hud tae leave her wi naethin. But mibby no, fur ah hink if ah'd asked her, ma mammy wid say we are her three best hings; Catherine and Elizabeth and
30 me.

Mary Ryan will collect in the compositions.

Ah walked roond the class, gaitherin in the bits a paper, lookin at each wan as ah picked it up. Aw they different kinds a haunwritin; squinty, straight, big or wee, different sizes and shapes on the page. Then ah picked up ma ain story wi its neat wee black drawins and
35 noticed ah hudny pit ma name on it. So ah drew a wee picture of masel wi a cheery face on it, pit ma story right on tap ae the pile and planted the whole lot doon in the centre of his desk.

MARKS

Questions

31. Look at lines 1—13.

    By referring to **one** example of language, explain how the writer makes it clear that Mary has tried hard to write a good story.   **2**

32. Look at lines 14—23.

    By referring to **one** example of language, explain how the writer suggests that Mary is thoughtful or considerate when choosing objects to take on the 'journey'.   **2**

33. Look at lines 24—30.

    By referring to **two** examples of language, explain what is revealed about the character of Mary's mother.   **4**

34. Look at lines 32—37.

    By referring to **two** examples, explain how the writer's use of language gives a clear sense of Mary's pride in her story.   **4**

35. By referring to this extract and to at least one other story, show how Donovan creates characters who are determined to do something.   **8**

[Turn over

SECTION 1 — SCOTTISH TEXT — 20 marks

PART C — SCOTTISH TEXT — POETRY

Text 1 — Poetry

If you choose this text you may not attempt a question on Poetry in Section 2.

Read the poem below and then attempt the following questions.

***The Way My Mother Speaks* by Carol Ann Duffy**

I say her phrases to myself
in my head
or under the shallows of my breath,
restful shapes moving.
5 *The day and ever. The day and ever.*

The train this slow evening
goes down England
browsing for the right sky,
too blue swapped for a cool grey.
10 For miles I have been saying
What like is it
the way I say things when I think.
Nothing is silent. Nothing is not silent.
What like is it.

15 Only tonight
I am happy and sad
like a child
who stood at the end of summer
and dipped a net
20 in a green, erotic pond. *The day
and ever. The day and ever.*
I am homesick, free, in love
with the way my mother speaks.

MARKS

Questions

36. Look at lines 1—5.

   By referring to **one** example of language, explain how the poet makes clear what the speaker is feeling.

   2

37. Look at lines 6—14.

   By referring to **two** examples of language, explain how the poet makes it clear that the journey is unsettling.

   4

38. Look at lines 15—20 ('Only tonight . . . erotic pond').

   By referring to **two** examples of language, explain how the poet presents the idea of growing up.

   4

39. Look at lines 22—23.

   Using your own words as far as possible, explain how the speaker feels at the end of the poem.

   You should make **two** key points.

   2

40. By referring to this poem and to at least one other by Duffy, show how the poet explores the idea of change.

   8

[Turn over

MARKS

OR

Text 2 — Poetry

If you choose this text you may not attempt a question on Poetry in Section 2.

Read the poem below and then attempt the following questions.

Glasgow Sonnet i by Edwin Morgan

A mean wind wanders through the backcourt trash.
Hackles on puddles rise, old mattresses
puff briefly and subside. Play-fortresses
of brick and bric-a-brac spill out some ash.
5 Four storeys have no windows left to smash,
but in the fifth a chipped sill buttresses
mother and daughter the last mistresses
of that black block condemned to stand, not crash.
Around them the cracks deepen, the rats crawl.
10 The kettle whimpers on a crazy hob.
Roses of mould grow from ceiling to wall.
The man lies late since he has lost his job,
smokes on one elbow, letting his coughs fall
thinly into an air too poor to rob.

Questions

41. Look at lines 1—4.

By referring to **two** examples of language, explain how the poet creates a negative first impression of the place.   4

42. Look at lines 5—8.

By referring to **two** examples of language, explain how the poet creates a sense of hopelessness.   4

43. Look at lines 9—14.

By referring to **two** examples of language, explain how the poet makes it clear the situation is extremely concerning.   4

44. By referring to this poem and to at least one other by Morgan, show how the poet explores painful experiences.   8

[Turn over for Text 3 — *Brooklyn cop* by Norman MacCaig]

DO NOT WRITE ON THIS PAGE

OR

Text 3 — Poetry

If you choose this text you may not attempt a question on Poetry in Section 2.

Read the poem below and then attempt the following questions.

Brooklyn cop by Norman MacCaig

Built like a gorilla but less timid,
thick-fleshed, steak-coloured, with two
hieroglyphs in his face that mean
trouble, he walks the sidewalk and the
5 thin tissue over violence. This morning,
when he said, 'See you, babe' to his wife,
he hoped it, he truly hoped it.
He is a gorilla
to whom 'Hiya, honey' is no cliché.

10 Should the tissue tear, should he plunge through
into violence, what clubbings, what
gunshots between Phoebe's Whamburger
and Louie's Place.

Who would be him, gorilla with a nightstick,
15 whose home is a place
he might, this time, never get back to?

And who would be who have to be
his victims?

MARKS

Questions

45. Look at lines 1—4 ('Built like . . . trouble').

By referring to **two** examples of language, explain how the poet creates a clear impression of the cop.

4

46. Look at lines 6—9.

By referring to **one** example of language, explain how the poet gives a clear sense of the cop's home life.

2

47. Look at lines 14—16.

By referring to **two** examples of language, explain how the poet highlights the threats that the cop faces daily.

4

48. Look at lines 17—18.

How effective do you find these lines as a conclusion to the poem? You should refer to **one** example from these lines, and to the language and/or ideas from the rest of the poem.

2

49. By referring to this poem and to at least one other by MacCaig, show how he explores human experience.

8

[Turn over

OR

Text 4 — Poetry

If you choose this text you may not attempt a question on Poetry in Section 2.

Read the extract below and then attempt the following questions.

My Grandmother's Houses by Jackie Kay

This extract is from sections 2 and 3 of the poem. In the first part of the poem, the poet has described her Grandmother's earlier tenement home and has fondly remembered childhood visits there as well as explaining her Grandmother's forced move to a 'high rise'.

2

But she still doesn't settle down;
even at 70 she cleans people's houses
for ten bob and goes to church on Sundays,
dragging me along to the strange place where the air
5 is trapped and ghosts sit at the altar.
My parents do not believe. It is down to her.
A couple of prayers. A hymn or two.
Threepenny bit in the collection hat.
A flock of women in coats and fussy hats
10 flapping over me like missionaries, and that is that,
until the next time God grabs me in Glasgow with Gran.

3

By the time I am seven we are almost the same height.
She still walks faster, rushing me down the High Street
till we get to her cleaning house. The hall is huge.
15 Rooms lead off like an octopus's arms.
I sit in a room with a grand piano, top open —
a one-winged creature, whilst my gran polishes
for hours. Finally bored I start to pick some notes,
oh can you wash a sailor's shirt oh can you wash and clean
20 till my gran comes running, duster in hand.
I told you don't touch anything. The woman comes too;
the posh one all smiles that make goosepimples
run up my arms. Would you like to sing me a song?
Someone's crying my Lord Kumbaya. Lovely, she says,
25 beautiful child, skin the colour of café au lait.
'Café oh what? Hope she's not being any bother.'
Not at all. Not at all. You just get back to your work.
On the way back to her high rise I see her
like the hunchback of Notre Dame. Everytime I crouch
30 over a comic she slaps me. Sit up straight.

She is on the ground floor of a high rise.
From her living-room you see ambulances,
screaming their way to the Royal Infirmary.

MARKS

Questions

50. Look at lines 1—11.

By referring to **two** examples of language, explain how the poet makes clear the speaker's feelings about going to church.   4

51. Look at lines 12—30.

By referring to **two** examples of language, explain what we learn about the relationship between the speaker and the Grandmother.   4

52. Look again at lines 12—30.

(a) By referring to **one** example of language, explain how the poet creates a clear impression of the house that the Grandmother cleans.   2

(b) By referring to **one** example of language, explain how the poet creates a clear impression of the attitude of the woman who lives there.   2

53. By referring to this extract and to at least one other poem by Kay, show how strong feelings are a feature of her poetry.   8

[END OF SECTION 1]

[Turn over

SECTION 2 — CRITICAL ESSAY — 20 marks

Attempt ONE question from the following genres — Drama, Prose, Poetry, Film and Television Drama, or Language.

Your answer must be on a different genre from that chosen in Section 1.

You should spend approximately 45 minutes on this section.

DRAMA

Answers to questions in this part should refer to the text and to such relevant features as characterisation, key scene(s), structure, climax, theme, plot, conflict, setting . . .

1. Choose a play in which one of the main characters has to face a difficulty.

   By referring to appropriate techniques, explain how the character's difficulty is explored.

2. Choose a play which deals with an important theme **or** issue.

   By referring to appropriate techniques, explain how the writer deals with this important theme or issue.

PROSE

Answers to questions in this part should refer to the text and to such relevant features as characterisation, setting, language, key incident(s), climax, turning point, plot, structure, narrative technique, theme, ideas, description . . .

3. Choose a novel **or** short story **or** work of non-fiction which explores a theme that interests you.

   By referring to appropriate techniques, explain how the writer makes this theme interesting.

4. Choose a novel **or** short story **or** work of non-fiction in which there is a character for whom you feel sympathy.

   By referring to appropriate techniques, explain how the writer makes you feel this way.

POETRY

Answers to questions in this part should refer to the text and to such relevant features as word choice, tone, imagery, structure, content, rhythm, rhyme, theme, sound, ideas . . .

5. Choose a poem which you found memorable.

   By referring to appropriate techniques, explain why you found the poem memorable.

6. Choose a poem which creates an atmosphere which is positive **or** sad **or** dramatic.

   By referring to appropriate techniques, explain how the poet creates this atmosphere.

FILM AND TELEVISION DRAMA

Answers to questions in this part should refer to the text and to such relevant features as use of camera, key sequence, characterisation, mise-en-scène, editing, setting, music/sound, special effects, plot, dialogue . . .

7. Choose a scene or sequence from a film **or** TV drama* in which an atmosphere of suspense **or** tension **or** horror is created.

   By referring to appropriate techniques, explain how this atmosphere is created.

8. Choose a film **or** TV drama which involves conflict.

   By referring to appropriate techniques, explain how this conflict is explored.

* 'TV drama' includes a single play, a series or a serial.

[Turn over

LANGUAGE

Answers to questions in this part should refer to the text and to such relevant features as register, accent, dialect, slang, jargon, vocabulary, tone, abbreviation . . .

9.   Consider an example of language which aims to persuade you to buy something new **or** change an aspect of your lifestyle **or** change your point of view.

   By referring to specific examples, explain how persuasive language is used effectively.

10.   Consider the distinctive language used by a group of people who use a particular dialect **or** specific vocabulary **or** any other language feature.

   By referring to specific examples, explain how the distinctive language is used.

[END OF SECTION 2]

[END OF QUESTION PAPER]

NATIONAL 5
Answers

NATIONAL 5 ENGLISH
2017

READING FOR UNDERSTANDING, ANALYSIS AND EVALUATION

1. 1 mark for any one reference; 1 mark for comment.

    Possible answers include:

    - "We played … every afternoon" suggests e.g. that it was their major pastime
    - "Sometimes other kids would join us" suggests e.g. occasionally they had more friends/bigger game/ community
    - "in the summer we never seemed to leave"/"game after game"/"sometimes until it got dark" suggests e.g. that they played constantly/all day
    - "endlessly" suggests e.g. enjoyment seemed never to stop
    - "absorbing" suggests e.g. that they found it fascinating/fulfilling/all-consuming
    - "dim glow of street lights" suggests e.g. nostalgia
    - "two litre bottle of orange squash" suggests e.g. simple childhood pleasures/nostalgia
    - "pass it from player to player" suggests e.g. camaraderie/innocence
    - "none of us deterred by [warmth]" suggests e.g. nothing would put them off
    - "it tasted good" suggests e.g. that the experience was pleasurable
      NB "good" on its own not sufficient.

2. Any four points.

    Glosses of:

    - "never made it onto the school team" e.g. was never picked/selected
      NB "team" need not be glossed.
    - "He kept trying"/"kept going to the trials"/"both at primary and senior school" e.g. persevered with opportunities for selection
    - "he was just off the pace" e.g. he was not quite fast/skilled enough
    - "He yearned to play" e.g. he longed to be part of/ play for the team
      NB Candidate must make reference to being in the team.
    - "He yearned … to progress" e.g. he longed to improve
    - "He yearned to … read out … (one of the honours of making the team)" e.g. he longed for his moment of glory

      *NB Candidate must refer to the intensity of the desire at least once if dealing with any of the **final three bullet points** (above).*

3. Any six points.

    Glosses of:

    - "98 per cent fail to make the transition (into professional football)"/"only a fraction made it (into professional football)" e.g. very few succeed

    - "Of those who made it into the district team, only a handful were picked by Reading, the local club"/"Perhaps none made it all the way to the top flight" e.g. even those who have some success didn't make it all the way/some progress doesn't necessarily mean success
    - "Many struggle to cope with rejection" e.g. many find it hard to come to terms with not being accepted
    - "many suffer anxiety" e.g. they are affected by stress
    - "many suffer … a loss of confidence" e.g. self-esteem/self-belief is undermined
    - "and, in some cases, depression" e.g. more serious mental health issues may develop
    - "These youngsters are often described as being "left on football's scrapheap" e.g. (inference) the process is heartless/rigorous/unfeeling
    - "it seems to me, though, that the number rejected is, in fact, far higher" e.g. those not selected exceeds number reported
    - "the sifting process starts from the first time you kick a ball at the local park" e.g. selection begins very early/there are many stages of filtering/selection
    - "the standard was high" e.g. the ability requirement is considerable
    - "I remember my heart beating out of my chest when the 'scouts' arrived" e.g. situation causes nerves/ pressure
    - "I was crushed by the disappointment" e.g. the distress (at failure) is overwhelming
    - "the race" e.g. the process is highly competitive
    - "… had only just started" e.g. the process is lengthy

4. - "Just as … so" structure may, but need not, be employed (1+1) e.g. just as there are many grains of sand on the beach so there are many people who don't succeed/are trying to succeed

    OR

    - any two areas of similarity. Ideas in common include multiplicity/identical or similar quality/anonymity/ insignificance/expendability/idea of being influenced by another/external/powerful force

5. 1 mark for any one reference; 1 mark for comment (×2).

    Possible answers include:

    Word choice:

    - "inevitable" makes clear the unavoidability of failure
    - "natural selection" or "evolution" makes clear e.g. survival of the fittest/that this is a process that has always existed
    - "part and parcel" — makes clear the essential nature/necessity of the process of selection

    Imagery:

    - "first lap"/"final straight"/reference to image of "race" — makes clear notion of a race/different stages of the process

      NB Do not reward a comment on "race" if the same word has been used as a reference.

Sentence structure:

- "But this is football."/"This is life."/short sentence(s) makes clear e.g. the fundamental/inarguable truth

- repetition of "this is" makes clear e.g. that this is a statement of fact/inescapable

- repetition of "failure is …" makes clear e.g. the fact that success is not universal

- "Without losers, there cannot be winners."/"Without pain, there cannot be joy."/"Without natural selection, there cannot be evolution."/reference to balance/contrast of opposites makes clear e.g. that life has ups and downs

- "Without losers, there cannot be winners. Without pain, there cannot be joy. Without natural selection, there cannot be evolution."/similarity/antithetical construction (within or in consecutive sentence(s))/parallel structure makes clear e.g. that life has ups and downs

- "Failure is not the opposite of progress; failure is part and parcel of progress."/use of semi-colon makes clear e.g. failure is crucial to moving on

  NB If no reference given, any comment cannot be rewarded.

  NB For full marks two different language features must be dealt with.

6. Any three points.

   Possible answers include:

   - "The skills are transparent" the criteria for success are obvious

   - "the opportunities exist" gives idea of chances being widely available

   - "There is no room for family favours" gives idea of lack of nepotism

   - "or cosy alliances" gives idea of lack of favourable treatment

   - "The best of the best shine through" gives idea of the most talented individuals do make it

   - "whether they are from a tough part of Liverpool, like Wayne Rooney, or raised in grinding poverty in Uruguay, like Luis Suárez" gives idea of irrelevance of background

7. Any five points.

   Glosses of:

   - "Youngsters who are educated and self-assured are likely to be better footballers, too" e.g. young people who have done well at school AND who are confident will perform more effectively

   - "The Ancient Greeks understood this only too well" e.g. it has been known for a long time

   - "(the humane idea) that the mind and body grow together" e.g. that emotional and physical development go hand in hand

   - "The German football system has embraced this truth, too" e.g. this is recognised abroad

   - "Such a cultural transformation needs to happen here, too" e.g. the lessons learned abroad should be considered in Britain

- "It is that we need to redefine our relationship with failure" e.g. we must reappraise how we view failure

- "not just in football but in life" e.g. we need to rethink how we deal with failure in areas other than football

- "losing is an essential (indeed, a beautiful) part of life" e.g. experiencing failure is necessary/natural

- "beautiful" e.g. failure can be viewed positively

- "the empowering idea that failure is less important, infinitely less so, than how we respond to it" e.g. how we react to failure is crucial/gives us strength/inspiration

- "Failing (to make the grade at football) is crushing" e.g. not being accepted (as a footballer) is devastating

- "It is natural to be sad" e.g. misery is to be expected/part of what we are

- "But it is also a pathway to a new reality" e.g. but leads us to a different life

  NB Candidates may use the word 'failure' in their response without penalty.

8. 1 mark for any one reference; 1 mark for comment.

   Possible answers include:

   - similarity of sentence openings/rule of three construction/"Tens of thousands … Hundreds of thousands … Tens of millions" highlights idea of scale/size of competition

   - "But" highlights the shift towards the positive side to failure

   - short sentence/"But this is not the end of life."/"It is merely the beginning." highlights that all is not lost

   - repetition of "a new"/rule of three construction/climactic structure/"a new dream, a new hope, a new way of finding meaning" highlights the possibility of a fresh start

     NB Do not accept list.

9. 1 mark for any one selection from lines 60–64; 1 mark for linked reference or explanation from elsewhere.

   Possible answers include:

   - reference to Mark/relates to earlier mentions of Mark

   - use of first person/relates to earlier use of first person

   - "failures (in football)" revisits important idea expressed by e.g. "never made it onto the school team", etc.

   - "so important, so trivial"/"Life is too short, too precious, to be derailed by failure" revisits important idea expressed by e.g. "failing to make the grade at football is crushing … but it is also the pathway to a new reality"

     NB Answer may address the idea of importance or triviality.

   - "never deterred him" revisits important idea expressed by e.g. "He kept trying"

   - "new dreams"/"new aspirations" repeats earlier use of word/idea

   - "accept" repeats earlier use of word/idea

   - "embrace" repeats earlier use of word/idea

- reference to a linguistic element from the final paragraph, e.g. repetition of word "too"/"we have"/sentence structure/short sentences/short paragraph(s) suggests emphatic nature of final summing up comments

  NB Do not reward a response that simply says 'it sums up the main ideas of the passage, etc.' unless the candidate goes on to explain what the main idea is.

CRITICAL READING
SECTION 1 — SCOTTISH TEXT
PART A — DRAMA – *Bold Girls* by Rona Munro

1. Any four points for 1 mark each.

   Candidates should use their own words.

   Possible answers include:

   - the women's lives can be disrupted by authoritative raids
   - they accept raids as part of life
   - the women's lives are mundane and a 'simple' night out can be looked forward to
   - the women speak frankly to each other
   - the women know their life style is not healthy
   - the omen are supportive of each other
   - Marie, Cassie and Nora are suspicious of Deirdre
   - there is tension between Cassie and Deirdre
   - Nora uses domesticity to comfort herself from the harshness of reality

2. 1 mark for reference; 1 mark for comment.

   Possible examples of humour include:

   - "It's the D.Ts" suggests irreverence/laughing at herself
   - "… the film stars have"/"Me and Joan Collins both" suggests exaggeration/mock self-importance
   - "… all the excitement" suggests sarcasm
   - "… would your manicure stand up to the closest inspection" suggests irony

3. (a) 1 mark for reference; 1 mark for comment.

   Possible answers include:

   - "Let's see Marie's hand there." suggests good humour between them
   - "Ah she's got a clear conscience." indicates respect for Marie
   - "Wired up but not plugged in." suggests humour/banter

   (b) 1 mark for reference; 1 mark for comment.

   Possible answers include:

   - "black wee heart"/"thieve the clothes"/"nail the wee snake down"/"… if it is Deirdre?" shows Cassie distrusts Deirdre
   - "It is." shows Deirdre stands up to Cassie
   - "I hope you've not taken a fancy … your eye" shows lack of trust

4. 1 mark for reference; 1 mark for comment.

   Possible answers include:

   - "What?" shows confrontation/confusion/defensiveness
   - "That I saw you before." shows accusation/confrontation

- "you're a lying hoor …" shows the anger/hostility Cassie feels towards Deirdre
- "… you never saw anything." shows defiance/threat/denial
- any part of "With a man. With him. With — " suggests build up to revelation
- identification of ellipsis suggests anticipation
- any reference to "Cassie lunges at her before she can get another word out" suggests desperation to stop her/aggression

5. Candidates are likely to include many different aspects of the mother–daughter theme.

   Possible areas for comment include:

   - despite Nora and Cassie's "bickering" they constantly support each other (especially with domestic hardships/challenges)
   - Hostilities due to memories of past relationship with father
   - Marie and Deirdre are likely to form a "mother/daughter" relationship despite the fact they are not directly blood relatives
   - Nora and Cassie "mother" Marie as they see her as a lone parent left in difficult circumstances (i.e. widowed and alone)
   - Deirdre and her biological mother are not close (as demonstrated by the fact that Deirdre is the victim of domestic violence perpetrated by her mother's latest boyfriend)

   Candidates may choose to answer in **bullet points** in this final question, or write a number of linked statements. There is **no requirement** to write a "mini essay".

   Up to 2 marks can be achieved for identifying elements of commonality as requested in the question. A further 2 marks can be achieved for **reference to the extract given.**

   4 additional marks can be awarded for similar references to **at least one other part of the text.**

   <u>In practice this means:</u>

   Identification of commonality (e.g. theme, central relationship, importance of setting, use of imagery, development in characterisation, use of personal experience, use of narrative style or any other key element …)

   From the extract:

   1 relevant reference to technique; 1 appropriate comment

   OR 1 relevant reference to idea; 1 appropriate comment

   OR 1 relevant reference to feature; 1 appropriate comment

   OR 1 relevant reference to text; 1 appropriate comment

   (maximum of 2 marks only for discussion of extract)

   from at **least one other part of the text:**

   as above (×2) for **up to 4 marks.**

PART A — DRAMA – *Sailmaker* by Alan Spence

6. 1 mark for identifying an aspect of Alec's attitude; 1 mark for supporting reference (×2).

   Possible answers include:

   - Alec is trying to understand his father e.g. by asking about his dad's reasons for gambling

- Alec has some admiration for his dad in the past e.g. memories of him making things/working as a Sailmaker
- Alec tries to encourage Davie e.g. to return to Sailmaking/to move elsewhere/to use his skills to create other products to sell
- Alec has accepted his dad for who he is/his likely relationship with his dad e.g. doesn't argue with Davie's (often unsatisfactory) responses/allows him to throw things of importance onto the fire

7. 1 mark for reference; 1 mark for comment (×2).

   Possible answers include:

   - "(Ah worked on the) Queen Mary (ye know)" e.g. suggests pride/sense of importance
   - "Worked on destroyers durin the war" suggests vivid memories (of usefulness)
   - Reference to list/"Made gun-covers, awnings, tarpaulins" suggests excitement at remembering detail/extent of work
   - "Made a shopping bag for yer mother"/"Made you a swing!"(1) suggests pleasure at creating gifts/ versatility of trade
   - "Wi a big sorta …" suggests detailed memory

8. 1 mark for reference; 1 mark for comment (×2).

   Possible answers include:

   - "Nae demand" suggests skills are not needed
   - "Was different durin the War" suggests times have changed
   - "(Been goin) downhill" circumstances have worsened
   - "Yards shuttin doon" suggests no market/ employment opportunities for his trade
   - "big empty space" place of work has literally gone
   - "covered wi weeds" suggests neglect
   - "redundancy money" suggests workers have been laid off/unemployment
   - "the manmade fibres"/"usin machines"/"Got lassies daein hauf the work" suggests original trade has changed beyond recognition
   - "Dead loss" suggests no hope for old trade

9. *Possible areas for comment include:*

   From the extract:

   - negative/pessimistic/lacking motivation
   - seen to be different before the death of his wife e.g. making bags and toys, working hard as an apprentice.
   - stage directions e.g. (shrugs)
   - negative language ("backed a loser right fae the start" and "Dead loss", etc.)

   From elsewhere:

   - answers will likely focus on Davie's downwards spiral from that start of the play triggered by his inability to cope with the death of his wife, which led to gambling and drinking
   - he also struggled to cope with being a single parent to Alec, and their home situation was often unsatisfactory (e.g. provision for meals and clothing as well as the generally untidy nature of the home)

- his employment situation changed from Sailmaker (before the play) to "tick man" to sweeper to eventually unemployed, all reflecting his decline in status/self-esteem
- he is seen as someone who always procrastinates (e.g. doing up the yacht, tidying the house) and who cannot move on (e.g. inability to be truthful about romantic interests)
- he is seen to be intelligent (e.g. discussing literature or religion) but he never uses this or his Sailmaking skills to try and improve his situation
- he lacks the ability to be pro-active about his situation and feels that he is always unlucky
- despite these failings, he constantly encourages Alec to look for something better in life and encourages him to find this through education and employment

Candidates may choose to answer in **bullet points** in this final question, or write a number of linked statements. There is **no requirement** to write a "mini essay".

Up to 2 marks can be achieved for identifying elements of commonality as requested in the question. A further 2 marks can be achieved for **reference to the extract given**.

4 additional marks can be awarded for similar references to **at least one other part of the text**.

In practice this means:

Identification of commonality (e.g. theme, central relationship, importance of setting, use of imagery, development in characterisation, use of personal experience, use of narrative style or any other key element …)

From the extract:

1 relevant reference to technique; 1 appropriate comment

OR 1 relevant reference to idea; 1 appropriate comment

OR 1 relevant reference to feature; 1 appropriate comment

OR 1 relevant reference to text; 1 appropriate comment

(maximum of 2 marks only for discussion of extract)

from at **least one other part of the text**:

as above (×2) for **up to 4 marks**.

PART A – DRAMA – *Tally's Blood* by Ann Marie Di Mambro

10. Candidates should make four key points for 1 mark each.

    Candidates may choose to make four separate summary points or may give both sides of two areas of disagreement.

    Possible answers include:

    - Rosinella thinks Hughie and Lucia are in love/ developing romantic feelings; but Massimo thinks they are just friends
    - Massimo thinks Lucia is upset about not getting to the wedding; but Rosinella thinks it's more than that
    - Massimo thinks there is no harm in her asking to go to the wedding; but Rosinella thinks it is concerning
    - Massimo thinks that Rosinella is too overbearing/ interfering/worrying too much; but Rosinella thinks she hasn't done enough to prevent this

- Rosinella is determined to prevent their relationship developing further; but Massimo does not want to get involved in it

11. 1 mark for reference; 1 mark for comment (×2).

    Possible answers include:

    - "She's to marry an Italian" suggests Rosinella's single mindedness/insistence
    - "I don't worry enough" suggests over protectiveness
    - "It's been going on before my eyes" suggests paranoia/suspicion
    - "It's bad enough he's fell for her" suggests her dislike of Hughie
    - "I'll soon put a stop to this before it starts" suggests her determination
    - "Italians are not interested …" suggests her prejudiced views
    - short sentences suggest her blunt/frank/straight to the point nature

12. 1 mark for identifying an attitude for each character; 1 mark for supporting reference (×2).

    Possible answers include:

    Rosinella:

    - "Are you forgetting what this country did …?" suggests anger/bitterness/inability to let go
    - "They took you" suggests sense of injustice
    - "as if you were a thief" suggests she feels Massimo's treatment was terrible/unforgivable
    - "I'll never get over it" suggests she feels that the trauma was too much to bear/she will hold a grudge forever

    Massimo:

    - "all I care about the war is that it's over" suggests he wants to move on from it/forget about it
    - "I lost ma faither, ma brother" suggests that he has a deep sadness/genuine grief at loss of family
    - "I lost … four years out ma life" suggests great sadness/resentment at losing his liberty
    - "everybody suffered"/"Not just us" suggests he accepts that grudges are pointless/the trauma is shared

13. *Possible areas for comment include:*

    From the extract:

    - Massimo is quiet, forgiving, unaware, private, patient, in love with Rosinella, etc.

    From elsewhere:

    - shows kindness e.g. by giving Hughie a job, offering him an ice cream van, giving Bridget money, etc.
    - shows patience e.g. with Rosinella's constant comments, interfering, bossing about, etc.
    - shows he is hard working e.g. works long hours in the shop while Rosinella and Lucia go out and spend, etc.
    - shows love towards Rosinella e.g. romantic story of their elopement (which he re-enacts at the end of the play), affectionately calls her "Rosie", etc.
    - suffers e.g. shop is attacked/has racist remarks made towards him, is taken hostage during the war, doesn't have a child of his own, etc.

Candidates may choose to answer in **bullet points** in this final question, or write a number of linked statements. There is **no requirement** to write a "mini essay".

Up to 2 marks can be achieved for identifying elements of commonality as requested in the question. A further 2 marks can be achieved for **reference to the extract given.**

4 additional marks can be awarded for similar references to at **least one other part of the text.**

In practice this means:

Identification of commonality (e.g. theme, central relationship, importance of setting, use of imagery, development in characterisation, use of personal experience, use of narrative style or any other key element …)

From the extract:

1 relevant reference to technique; 1 appropriate comment

OR 1 relevant reference to idea; 1 appropriate comment

OR 1 relevant reference to feature; 1 appropriate comment

OR 1 relevant reference to text; 1 appropriate comment

(maximum of 2 marks only for discussion of extract)

from at **least one other part of the text:**

as above (×2) for **up to 4 marks.**

PART B — PROSE — *The Cone-Gatherers* by Robin Jenkins

14. Any four points for 1 mark each.

    Candidates should use their own words as far as possible.

    Possible answers include:

    - no electric lighting
    - there is not much natural light — reference to a single window
    - there is little furniture — a box for a table/only two beds
    - there are no soft furnishings — newspaper is used instead of a tablecloth
    - they make the best of what they have
    - the cones being burned — this creates a pleasant smell in the hut
    - they have a simple routine e.g. they prepare the vegetables the evening before
    - they prepare and eat their meal without washing/don't change their clothes
    - there is little conversation/they are content with the silence/they are exhausted
    - they pass the time doing simple things e.g. they have an unvarying routine

15. 1 mark for reference; 1 mark for comment (×2).

    Possible answers include:

    - "against his will" suggests that Duror is forced to recognise something positive about the cone-gatherers/they are at one with nature
    - "final defeat" — word choice suggests that Duror is somehow seeking victory over the cone-gatherers/thinks he is superior

Possible answers include:

- 'trained' suggests e.g. cats were taught (what to do)
- 'pests' suggests e.g. cats got rid of destructive creatures
- 'lost' suggests e.g. without cats knowledge would have disappeared
- '(four-legged) protectors' suggests e.g. cats looked after Egyptian writing/were the guardians of the writing
- 'guarding (the temples)' suggests e.g. cats defended Egyptian writing
- 'intruders' suggests e.g. cats stopped invaders

7. 1 mark for any one reference; 1 mark for comment (×2), for a maximum of 4 marks.

Possible answers include:

Word choice:

- 'cartoonesque'/'Tom and Jerry' suggests e.g. he disagrees with the stereotypical/unrealistic/representation of cats
- 'dumb (cat)' suggests e.g. that the writer has the opposite view/is used in an ironic sense
- '(always) foiled' suggests e.g. that writer thinks whatever the cat does it cannot win
- 'tiny adversary' suggests e.g. ridiculous elevation of mouse/is used in an ironic sense
- '(little) pests' suggests e.g. mice should be considered as undesirable creatures
- 'gnawing'/'gnawing on our possessions' suggests e.g. continuous destruction/suggests that mice ruin our things
- 'spreading'/'spreading disease' suggests e.g. mice are causing harm everywhere/are dangerous (to our health)
- 'unfair' suggests e.g. cats are unjustly treated

Sentence structure:

- 'It's unfair.'/short sentence emphasises e.g. writer's opinion that cats are treated without due respect
- contrast of long and short sentences gives e.g. emphatic weight to writer's opinion that treatment of cats is unjust

Tone:

- reference to appropriate tone e.g. 'like we're supposed to' creates a mocking tone

8. Any five points, for a maximum of 5 marks.

Possible answers include:

- 'Look to Russia' glossed by e.g. it all started in Russia OR 'decree issued by Empress Elizabeth' glossed by e.g. (cats were subject to) a special order
- 'to protect the treasures contained within (the Museum) from rats' glossed by e.g. cats were employed to stop rats from ruining the valuables (of the museum)
  NB Both 'protect' and 'treasures' must be glossed here

- 'Europeans still sure that rats caused the Black Death' glossed by e.g. rats were blamed for the Plague OR 'rat catchers unable to stop rodents from overrunning' glossed by e.g. the rat population was out of control
  NB 'caused' must be glossed
- 'the British government started to encourage libraries to keep cats in order to bring down populations of (book-loving) vermin' glossed by e.g. the use of cats was recommended in UK libraries to deal with the rats
  NB 'encouraged' must be glossed
- 'It made sense that bookshop owners would also employ the four-legged security guards …' glossed by e.g. cats were then brought in to protect bookshops too
- 'Cats were easy to find' glossed by e.g. it was straightforward to come by cats OR 'all you had to do was feed them as compensation' glossed by e.g. cats don't require any special treatment/much looking after
  NB 'easy' must be glossed
- '(And once cats were invited …) they never really left.' glossed by e.g. cats stayed on in libraries/bookshops

9. 1 mark for any one selection; 1 mark for comment.

NB do not reward a response which simply says 'it sums up the main ideas of the passage etc' unless the candidate goes on to explain what the main idea is.

Possible answers include:

- 'cats are quiet and want to be left alone'/'long for solitude' repeats the idea of e.g. 'goes right back to sleep'
- 'It began as a working relationship' repeats the idea of e.g. 'cats were trained'
- 'became something more than that'/'something deeper' repeats the idea of e.g. 'Cats held a special place in Egyptian society'
- 'became integral to the bookshop experience' repeats the idea of e.g. 'the photogenic spirit of the place' OR repeats the idea of e.g. 'Why do cats love bookshops?'/the title
- 'a small part of why … local shop (than buy online)' repeats the idea of the presence of cats in bookshops
- 'cat prowling around' repeats the idea of e.g. 'four-legged protectors'
- 'a big part of what makes these stores great'/'main attraction' repeats the idea of e.g. 'five seconds to impress him'/'apex of domesticated pets', etc.
- 'along with, you know' repeats humorous tone of paragraph one
- 'if you asked a cat' repeats the idea of e.g. 'once cats were invited into bookshops'/writer's humanisation of cats/second person address engages reader OR repeats the idea of e.g. 'Why do cats love bookshops?'/the title
- 'god-like status' repeats the idea of e.g. 'Egyptians worshipped them'/'the sort of treatment they received in the time of pharaoh'

CRITICAL READING

SECTION 1 – SCOTTISH TEXT

PART A – DRAMA – *Bold Girls* by Rona Munro

1. Any four points for 1 mark each.

    Possible answers include:

    - Nora criticises Cassie for her story telling
    - Nora bemoans the past
    - Nora is upset at the loss of her material for her soft furnishings
    - Marie reassures Nora
    - the tension between Cassie and Nora increases when Cassie does not answer Nora
    - Nora says she will secure credit under false pretences to buy new material
    - Marie warns Cassie that if she leaves, it will devastate Nora
    - Cassie says that Nora is stronger than she seems
    - Cassie threatens revenge on Deirdre
    - Marie assures Cassie that Deirdre will get her comeuppance
    - Cassie asks Marie how she remains so positive about her life
    - Cassie says she is no good

2. 1 mark for reference; 1 mark for comment (×2), for a maximum of 4 marks.

    Possible answers include:

    - repetition of "lost" suggests she really cares about it
    - repetition of "gone" suggests hopelessness
    - "Months" suggests how long she has been looking forward to this
    - "dreaming of the glow" suggests how affectionate she feels about the remnant
    - "Never" suggests her vision is unattainable
    - "lovely" suggests how she imagined the room to be as perfect as possible
    - use of short sentences suggests Nora speaks in an emotional voice
    - "And he's lost it" suggests her anger
    - use of stage direction/"Getting tearful in her turn" suggests Nora is going to cry
    - use of question suggests that she needs reassurance

3. 1 mark for reference; 1 mark for comment (×2), for a maximum of 4 marks.

    Possible answers include:

    - Nora becomes more argumentative towards Cassie "drawing herself up"/"She snatches up her drink and takes an angry gulp"
    - Cassie tries to avoid the confrontation with Nora "Cassie doesn't look at Nora"/"looking up at Nora"
    - Nora starts to become upset "She is getting tearful in her turn"
    - Nora finds Cassie's words incredulous "Nora stares at her for a moment, then she nods"

    - Marie realises that Cassie is at a crisis point and offers her more alcohol "Marie puts the gin bottle down in front of Cassie"
    - Cassie drinks quickly as she is on edge "Cassie helps herself to another drink"
    - Marie defiantly puts Michael's picture back up on the wall "… she goes and rehangs it carefully"

4. *Possible areas for comment include:*

    Extract:

    - Nora loudly criticises Cassie e.g. 'There's no end to your wild tales Cassie!'
    - Nora is assertive e.g. 'Well I'm going up the town tomorrow.'
    - Cassie threatens revenge e.g. 'There's a waitress up that club will be walking around without her hair tomorrow if I can find her.'

    Elsewhere:

    - connotations of bravery and resilience – the women exist in a harsh setting
    - connotations of risk taking behaviour (demonstrated by Cassie)
    - connotations of self-confidence
    - connotations of humour
    - the women have domestic and financial hardships to face
    - the women face harsh critics in their community

    Candidates may choose to answer in **bullet points** in this final question, or write a number of linked statements. There is **no requirement** to write a 'mini essay'.

    Up to 2 marks can be achieved for identifying elements of **commonality** as identified in the question.

    A further 2 marks can be achieved for **reference to the extract given.**

    4 additional marks can be awarded for similar references to **at least one other text/part of the text** by the writer.

    <u>In practice this means:</u>

    Identification of commonality (2) (e.g. theme, central relationship, importance of setting, use of imagery, development in characterisation, use of personal experience, use of narrative style, or any other key element …)

    From the extract:

    1 relevant reference to technique; 1 appropriate comment

    OR 1 relevant reference to idea; 1 appropriate comment

    OR 1 relevant reference to feature; 1 appropriate comment

    OR 1 relevant reference to text; 1 appropriate comment

    (maximum of 2 marks only for discussion of extract)

    from at **least one other text/part of the text:**

    as above (×2) for **up to 4 marks**

PART A — DRAMA — *Sailmaker* by Alan Spence

5. 1 mark for reference; 1 mark for comment (×2), up to a maximum of 4 marks.

   Possible answers include:

   - "Screw the heid" suggests that he is not himself
   - "ah dae ma best" suggests he recognises that he is trying to sort things out
   - "it's just …" suggests he is making excuses
   - "…" suggests unfinished explanation
   - "Hard on yer own" suggests he is struggling to cope
   - "Naw ye don't know/Naebody knows (unless they've been through it)" suggests only some people understand his current problems
   - "(Quieter)" suggests lack of confidence
   - "Comin hame's the worst/The boy's oot playin/Hoose is empty" suggests loneliness
   - "gets on top of ye" suggests being overwhelmed
   - Reference to furniture watching him suggests paranoia/lack of rational thought
   - "Maybe ah'm going aff ma heid!" suggests concern over mental health/suggests belittling his fear
   - "take a while" suggests difficulty of issue to be dealt with
   - "(take a while) tae get over it" acknowledgement that there is an issue
   - "If ah ever dae" suggests enormity of problem to be faced

6. 1 mark for reference; 1 mark for comment (×2), up to a maximum of 4 marks.

   Possible answers include:

   - "How ye doin wee yin?" suggests empathy
   - "What's this ye've got?/(Picks up yacht)" suggests he's taking an interest in Alec
   - "Ah could paint it if ye like" suggests Billy is proactive
   - "Should come up really nice" suggests optimism
   - "Ah'll take it away wi me/Get it done this week" suggests urgency
   - "Nae bother!" suggests helpfulness
   - reference to possible finished appearance of yacht suggests practical ability/skill/imagination/ resourcefulness/creativity …

7. 1 mark for reference; 1 mark for comment.

   Possible answers include:

   Alec

   "It'll be dead real, eh?" suggests excitement/gratitude

   Reference to question mark suggests interest

   Davie

   "Away tae Never Never Land!" suggests sarcasm/lack of enthusiasm/dismissiveness

   Reference to exclamation mark suggests sarcasm.

8. 1 mark for each point, up to a maximum of 2 marks.

   Possible answers include:

   - Symbolises Davie's inaction
   - Symbolises Billy's action
   - represents Alec's (childhood) belief in Davie
   - symbolises Alec and Davie's relationship
   - symbolises Davie's previous trade
   - reference to colours/football associations
   - symbolises Alec's childhood
   - symbolises freedom/hope/new horizons
   - yacht represents conflict

9. Possible areas for comment include:

   Extract:

   Billy could be seen to be interfering in Davie's relationship with Alec e.g. "He'll get on a lot better if you screw the heid, right?"

   Billy shows interest in/concern for Alec e.g. "how ye doin wee yin/what's this ye've got?"

   Elsewhere:

   Billy is helpful and tries to give practical advice to Alec and to Davie (in terms of their domestic situation as well as possible employment …).

   The relationship between Billy and Ian (which is a close one) is in direct contrast to the relationship between Alec and Davie because their relationship worsens.

   The family interest in football is at the centre of many interactions between the main characters.

   There is some role reversal because Alec carries out the traditional 'adult' chores/functions. 8 Candidates may choose to answer in **bullet points** in this final question, or write a number of linked statements. There is **no requirement** to write a 'mini essay'.

   The yacht represents the breakdown of the family relationship between Alec and Davie and Billy's attempts to fix it up show that he tries to help mend the family relationship.

   Up to 2 marks can be achieved for identifying elements of **commonality** as identified in the question.

   A further 2 marks can be achieved for **reference to the extract given.**

   4 additional marks can be awarded for similar references to **at least one other text/part of the text** by the writer.

   In practice this means:

   Identification of commonality (2) (e.g. theme, central relationship, importance of setting, use of imagery, development in characterisation, use of personal experience, use of narrative style, or any other key element …)

   From the extract:

   1 × relevant reference to technique
   1 × appropriate comment

   OR 1 × relevant reference to idea
   1 × appropriate comment

   References to the past are used to contextualise current strains in the characters' relationships (e.g. death of the mother; unemployment from the sail-making trade …).

   Davie is a traditionalist, in terms of family roles/ aspirations, whereas Alec breaks from these traditions (e.g. with further education).

   Family attitudes to education highlight the differences between Ian and Alec and Alec and Davie.

OR 1 × relevant reference to feature
1 × appropriate comment

OR 1 × relevant reference to text
1 × appropriate comment

(maximum of 2 marks only for discussion of extract)

from at **least one other text/part of the text:**

as above (×2) for **up to 4 marks**

PART A − DRAMA − *Tally's Blood* **by Ann Marie Di Mambro**

10. 1 mark for reference; 1 mark for comment (×2), up to a maximum of 4 marks.

    Possible answers include:

    - "You better watch these lassies" suggests warning him off
    - *"(Franco scoffs)"* suggests that he is dismissive
    - "Who is it anyway?" suggests loaded question
    - "This is not "anybody"" suggests he is defensive
    - *"(Disapproving)"* suggests critical, judgemental etc
    - "What if she is?" suggests challenging statement

11. (a) 1 mark for reference; 1 mark for comment.

    Possible answers include:

    - "six or seven weans"/*"(shocked)"*/"Eight weans!" suggests her surprise at the size of the family
    - "She cannie even look after them right" suggests that she feels the family is neglected/not cared for properly
    - "It's no fair" suggests that she is jealous of Bridget's family

    (b) 1 mark for reference; 1 mark for comment.

    Possible answers include:

    - "Eight." suggests a neutral statement of fact/not critical
    - "They're a great family" suggests he has admiration for the family
    - "Really close" suggests he thinks the family have a good bond

12. 1 mark for reference; 1 mark for comment (×2), up to a maximum of 4 marks.

    Possible answers include:

    - "I wasn't looking" suggests he is serious about Bridget/not hoping to meet someone else
    - "I told you, Rosinella, I've got someone" suggests seriousness/determination/loyalty
    - "What if I am?" suggests he has his own opinions/is independent
    - "You know nothing about Bridget" suggests the depth of his feelings for her
    - *"(Indignant)"* suggests he can become angry/irritated
    - "Good looking"/"a good kisser"/"a good dancer" suggests he is self-assured/confident
    - "Oh they like that alright"/"they're all over me" suggests he is conceited
    - "you've got the warm blood"/"it's one thing to play around with them" suggests prior romantic liaisons

13. Possible areas for comment include:

    Extract:

    - Rosinella shows her prejudice against Scottish girls e.g. 'These Scotch girls they're all the same.'
    - Rosinella is resentful of the fact that she has not been able to have children of her own e.g. 'Twelve years I've been married – and nothing.'

    Elsewhere:

    - Rosinella is shown as caring in that she offers Lucia a new life in Scotland
    - Rosinella is seen to spoil Lucia
    - Rosinella comes into conflict with her husband Massimo about Lucia's upbringing
    - Rosinella is proud of her Italian heritage
    - Rosinella tries to ensure that Franco and Bridget won't be together
    - Rosinella suffers (when, for example, Massimo is imprisoned)
    - Rosinella shows signs of hypocrisy over romantic relationships

    Candidates may choose to answer in **bullet points** in this final question, or write a number of linked statements. There is **no requirement** to write a 'mini essay'.

    Up to 2 marks can be achieved for identifying elements of **commonality** as identified in the question.

    A further 2 marks can be achieved for **reference to the extract given.**

    4 additional marks can be awarded for similar references to **at least one other text/part of the text** by the writer.

    In practice this means:

    Identification of commonality (2) (e.g. theme, central relationship, importance of setting, use of imagery, development in characterisation, use of personal experience, use of narrative style, or any other key element ...)

    From the extract:

    1 × relevant reference to technique
    1 × appropriate comment

    OR 1 × relevant reference to idea
    1 × appropriate comment

    OR 1 × relevant reference to feature
    1 × appropriate comment

    OR 1 × relevant reference to text
    1 × appropriate comment

    (maximum of 2 marks only for discussion of extract)

    from at **least one other text/part of the text:**

    as above (×2) for **up to 4 marks**

PART B − PROSE − *The Cone-Gatherers* **by Robin Jenkins**

14. 1 mark for reference; 1 mark for comment (×2), up to a maximum of 4 marks.

    Possible answers include:

    - "Put it back, Calum," suggests Neil is in charge
    - "Would it be alright if ..." suggests Calum is anxious to receive permission from Neil

- "It would be stealing"/"Get your jacket ... hold it in front of the fire." suggests Neil assumes parental role
- "Calum was delighted"/"I'm not telling," suggests Calum is eager to please Neil

15. 1 mark for reference; 1 mark for comment (×2), up to a maximum of 4 marks.

Possible answers include:

- "other noises outside" suggests disturbance
- "drumming of the rain" suggests ominous sound
- reference to use of colon suggests threatening noises are identified
- "dog's bark" suggests aggression
- "scratching on it as of paws" suggests fear of the unknown
- "stared towards the door" suggests fear
- "the lady cry out" suggests alarming exclamation
- "key rattled in the lock" suggests getting closer/ person outside coming in
- "The door was flung open" suggests dramatic entrance
- "loudest peal of thunder" suggests terrifying noise

16. 1 mark for reference; 1 mark for comment (×2), up to a maximum of 4 marks.

Possible answers include:

- "Neil did not know what to do or say" suggests Neil is at a loss/very confused
- "silent" suggests he doesn't know what to say
- "abjectness" suggests loss of pride
- "betrayal of himself" suggests he feels he is not giving an account of himself or Calum
- "All his vows ..." suggests he feels he is going back on all his intentions/promises regarding Calum
- "rheumatism tortured him"/"fire had been pressed into ..." suggests he is suffering intensely
- "punish him as he deserved" suggests he is full of self-loathing
- "He could not lift his head" suggests he is unable to face the situation
- "lifetime of frightened submissiveness" suggests he is acutely aware of his place in the 'class system'
- "Suddenly" suggests shock/surprise (that Calum is speaking)

17. Possible areas for comment include:

Extract:

- Neil's almost paternal care for Calum: e.g. "Neil went over to attend to the fire."
- Neil's acute awareness of social class/rank e.g. "A life of frightened submissiveness."
- Calum's innocence e.g. "I would put it back."

Elsewhere:

- Calum is linked with animals and nature. He is at home in the trees
- Calum is not resentful of his own appearance. This is in direct contrast with Duror's view
- Calum is generally seen to represent innocence

- Neil makes sacrifices in order to care for his brother
- Neil has a rational view of the world and is less interested in nature than Calum
- Neil believes the war will be beneficial to people like him

Candidates may choose to answer in **bullet points** in this final question, or write a number of linked statements. There is **no requirement** to write a 'mini essay'.

Up to 2 marks can be achieved for identifying elements of **commonality** as identified in the question.

A further 2 marks can be achieved for **reference to the extract given.**

4 additional marks can be awarded for similar references to **at least one other text/part of the text** by the writer.

<u>In practice this means:</u>

Identification of commonality (2) (e.g. theme, central relationship, importance of setting, use of imagery, development in characterisation, use of personal experience, use of narrative style, or any other key element ...)

From the extract:

1 × relevant reference to technique
1 × appropriate comment

OR 1 × relevant reference to idea

1 × appropriate comment

OR 1 × relevant reference to feature
1 × appropriate comment

OR 1 × relevant reference to text
1 × appropriate comment

(maximum of 2 marks only for discussion of extract)

from at **least one other text/part of the text:**

as above (×2) for **up to 4 marks**

PART B — PROSE — *The Testament of Gideon Mack* **by James Robertson**

18. 1 mark for reference; 1 mark for comment (×2), up to a maximum of 4 marks.

Possible answers include:

- short first sentence is dramatic
- "sweating" suggests nervousness
- "seething" suggests intensity
- "wrecked" suggests overcome with anxiety
- "afraid" suggests anxiety
- "provoked" suggests disturbed
- "crisis" suggests importance of situation
- "I paced ..." suggests stress
- "as if in contact with an electric fence" suggesting agitation
- contradiction in wanting to go but afraid to suggests indecision
- "(I paced ...) in and out of every room, up and down the stairs" suggests incessant walking, restlessness etc
- says he wants to go for a run "to calm down" suggests he is in a heightened state

19. 1 mark for reference; 1 mark for comment.

Possible answers include:

- "I've had a good look round." suggests enthusiasm
- "Is this an awkward moment?" suggests sensitivity/ social awareness
- "You wouldn't like to come for a walk instead?" suggests persistence
- "I can't say I understood everything" suggests modesty
- "it was quite thought-provoking" suggests intellectual curiosity
- "while I was looking down through that window" suggests nosiness

20. 1 mark for each point, up to a maximum of 2 marks.

Possible answers include:

- he sees it as fate/the influence of the Stone
- going there will allow him to discuss things with her
- if she saw the Stone, he would talk to John and Elsie
- if she didn't see the Stone, he would admit madness or a breakdown and seek help

21. 1 mark for reference; 1 mark for comment (×2), up to a maximum of 4 marks.

Possible answers include:

- "I wouldn't be back (for nearly a week)" suggests longer than anticipated absence
- "Nor could I have foreseen" suggests mysterious event
- "utterly transformed" suggests unexpectedly huge change
- "Nor indeed … could I have guessed" suggests complete surprise
- repetition of "Nor" emphasises his uncertainty
- "but her dog" suggests suspense/anticipation

22. Possible areas for comment include:

Extract:

Reference made to curiosity about Keldo woods and the cave at the Black Jaws, e.g. "take her to Keldo woods, and show her the Stone."

Elsewhere:

- the manse at Ochtermill, linked to Gideon's origins, his early family influences, and the theme of religion
- Keldo woods, linked with the supernatural, local superstitions, and Gideon's 'inner life'/psychology, etc.
- the Black Jaws, linked with Gideon's transformational meeting with the Devil

Candidates may choose to answer in **bullet points** in this final question, or write a number of linked statements. There is **no requirement** to write a 'mini essay'.

Up to 2 marks can be achieved for identifying elements of **commonality** as identified in the question.

A further 2 marks can be achieved for **reference to the extract given.**

4 additional marks can be awarded for similar references to **at least one other text/part of the text** by the writer.

In practice this means:

Identification of commonality (2) (e.g. theme, central relationship, importance of setting, use of imagery, development in characterisation, use of personal experience, use of narrative style, or any other key element …)

From the extract:

1 × relevant reference to technique
1 × appropriate comment

OR 1 × relevant reference to idea
1 × appropriate comment

OR 1 × relevant reference to feature
1 × appropriate comment

OR 1 × relevant reference to text
1 × appropriate comment

(maximum of 2 marks only for discussion of extract)

from at **least one other text/part of the text:**

as above (× 2) for **up to 4 marks**

PART B — PROSE — *Kidnapped* **by Robert Louis Stevenson**

23. 1 mark for reference; 1 mark for comment (×2), up to a maximum of 4 marks.

Possible answers include:

- "he could bear it no longer" suggests that there has been previous tension
- "this is no way for two friends (to take a small accident)" suggests there has been a difference of opinion
- "I'm sorry" suggests remorse
- "ye'd better say it" suggests threatening/challenging comment
- "I have nothing" denial suggests something unsaid
- "disconcerted" suggests flustered
- "I was meanly pleased" suggests David is enjoying Alan's discomfort
- "of course, ye were to blame" suggests David thinks Alan was at fault
- "coolly" suggests tense atmosphere between the pair

24. 1 mark for reference; 1 mark for comment (×2), up to a maximum of 4 marks.

Possible answers include:

- "This pierced me like a sword" suggests that he was wounded/really hurt
- "lay bare" suggests vulnerability
- "I cried" suggests strong emotion
- "Do you think I am one to turn my back …" suggests he is indignant
- "cast it up to me" suggest defensiveness
- repetition of the word "you" suggests frustration

25. 1 mark for reference; 1 mark for comment (×2), up to a maximum of 4 marks.

Possible answers include:

- appropriate reference conciliatory
- appropriate reference worried

- appropriate reference guilty conscience
- appropriate reference concerned
- appropriate reference manipulative

26. Possible areas for comment include:

Extract:

Example of friendship being strained in the extract, but at the same time we can see their genuine caring heart of their friendship for each other amidst the strained atmosphere, e.g. "This pierced me like a sword"

Elsewhere:

- Alan & David's friendship is surprising as they come from opposite political backgrounds and beliefs
- their friendship is challenged throughout the novel
- friendship established when David overhears crew of *Covenant* planning to overthrow Alan Breck and David warns Alan
- violent fight in the Round-House of the Covenant is where David helps Alan
- Alan gives David a silver button as a token of gratitude/friendship for David's actions
- murder of Red Fox puts grave doubts in David's head about Alan's character and their continuing friendship
- Alan and David continue on their journey and therefore their friendship is maintained
- Alan loses all their money at a game of cards and this puts pressure on their friendship
- David challenges Alan to a duel – Alan refuses and they make up
- when they arrive in Edinburgh, Alan helps David gain his rightful title and inheritance
- with the help of Rankeillor, David gives Alan money to get back to France
- David and Alan, at the end of the novel, struggle to part due to their strong friendship

Candidates may choose to answer in **bullet points** in this final question, or write a number of linked statements. There is **no requirement** to write a 'mini essay'.

Up to 2 marks can be achieved for identifying elements of **commonality** as identified in the question.

A further 2 marks can be achieved for **reference to the extract given.**

4 additional marks can be awarded for similar references to **at least one other text/part of the text** by the writer.

In practice this means:

Identification of commonality (2) (e.g. theme, central relationship, importance of setting, use of imagery, development in characterisation, use of personal experience, use of narrative style, or any other key element ...)

From the extract:

1 × relevant reference to technique
1 × appropriate comment

OR 1 × relevant reference to idea
1 × appropriate comment

OR 1 × relevant reference to feature
1 × appropriate comment

OR 1 × relevant reference to text
1 × appropriate comment

(maximum of 2 marks only for discussion of extract)

from at **least one other text/part of the text:**

as above (×2) for **up to 4 marks**

PART B – PROSE – *The Red Door* by Iain Crichton Smith

27. 1 mark for reference; 1 mark for comment (×2), up to a maximum of 4 marks.

Possible answers include:

- "stared" suggests he can't make sense of it
- "deep caves" suggests the unknown
- "seemed to be drawn inside it" suggests the door has almost supernatural power
- "veins and passages" suggests hidden parts/secrets
- "magic (door)" suggests it is irrational/unexpected/ unexplained/impressive
- "deep red light" suggests unexpected brightness/ intense colour
- "appear alive" suggests door has life of its own
- "very odd and very puzzling" suggests lack of explanation
- "scratching his head" suggests confusion caused by the door
- "couldn't see himself in it" suggests unnatural quality
- "sucked into it" suggests odd power/attraction
- "different" suggests stands out

28. One mark for each point.

Possible answers include:

- he loves the door
- he is not annoyed that it has been painted
- he is impressed by (the idea of) the door

29. 1 mark for reference; 1 mark for comment.

Possible answers include:

- "childlikeness" suggests the beginning of a life/sense of wonder
- "stirring within him" suggests new birth/emergence
- "rousing" suggests awakening/change
- "new day" suggests a beginning
- "joyously" suggests excitement (at new beginning)
- "early" suggests the beginning of a journey

30. 1 mark for reference; 1 mark for comment (×2), up to a maximum of 4 marks.

Possible answers include:

- "sparkling frost" suggests attractive, magical, appealing surroundings
- "new" suggests freshness
- "diamonds" suggests something precious
- "glittered" suggests attractive/appealing
- "millions of them" suggests abundance
- "shone bravely" suggests having an admirable quality

- "pride" suggests pleased with what it has achieved
- "spirit" suggests enthusiasm/energy
- "emerged" suggests birth/renewal
- "brightly" suggests fresh/appealing
- "let me live my own life" suggests independence/aspiration

31. Possible areas for comment include:

Extract:

Themes from extract e.g.

Individual vs conformity, restrictive nature of community/environment.

Elsewhere:

- *Mother and Son*
  themes of freedom/lack of freedom/restrictive nature of mother and son relationship

- *The Telegram*
  themes of restrictive nature of small town community – treatment of the 'thin woman,' intrusive/restrictive nature of the community as a group

- *The Painter*
  themes of restrictive nature of community – William has to escape the community to gain freedom/creativity

- *In Church*
  Lack of freedom/entrapment caused by war. Candidates may choose to answer in **bullet points** in this final question, or write a number of linked statements. There is **no requirement** to write a 'mini essay'

Up to 2 marks can be achieved for identifying elements of **commonality** as identified in the question.

A further 2 marks can be achieved for **reference to the extract given.**

4 additional marks can be awarded for similar references to **at least one other text/part of the text** by the writer.

<u>In practice this means:</u>

Identification of commonality (2) (e.g. theme, central relationship, importance of setting, use of imagery, development in characterisation, use of personal experience, use of narrative style, or any other key element …)

From the extract:

1 × relevant reference to technique
1 × appropriate comment

OR 1 × relevant reference to idea
1 × appropriate comment

OR 1 × relevant reference to feature
1 × appropriate comment

OR 1 × relevant reference to text
1 × appropriate comment

(maximum of 2 marks only for discussion of extract)

from at **least one other text/part of the text:**

as above (×2) for **up to 4 marks**

PART B – PROSE – *Away in a Manger* **by Anne Donovan**

32. 1 mark for reference; 1 mark for comment.

Possible answers include:

- "Are you cauld?" suggests a reason to postpone trip
- "A vision of warmth"/"a fire"/"a mug of hot tea" suggests more attractive options
- "We could come back"/"another night" suggest an attempt to cancel/postpone trip
- "Naw, Mammy, naw"/"we cannae go hame noo"/"we're nearly there"/"you promised" suggests Amy senses Sandra's reluctance
- "All right, we'll go." suggests giving in, but not keen

33. 1 mark for reference; 1 mark for comment (×2), up to a maximum of 4 marks.

Possible answers include:

- "gaun on aboot the lights (for weeks)" suggests Sandra is tired of hearing about the decorations, etc
- "ower and done wi" suggests she wants the season to be finished
- "she was sick of it all" suggests that was bored/weary with the season
- "opened longer and longer" suggests she is tired of her shop's extended opening hours
- "trippin ower wan another" suggests she hates the busy shops/festive season crowds
- "everybody in a bad mood" suggests she hates the collective misery
- "trachled (wi parcels)" suggests she dislikes the exhaustion of Christmas shopping
- "those bloody Christmas records" suggests she dislikes the seasonal music
- "extra hours"/"old bag of a supervisor"/"extra couple of hours"/"hit her ower the heid …" suggest she doesn't like the additional work pressures that the season brings

34. 1 mark for each point.

Possible answers include:

- wants to please her (by taking her to see the decorations)
- cares about her appearance (by buying her nice clothes)
- wants the best for her
- she is full of admiration for the way she looks
- cares about her manners, etc.

35. 1 mark for reference; 1 mark for comment (×2), up to a maximum of 4 marks.

Possible answers include:

- "the cauld evaporated" suggests the cold (magically) seems to disappear
- "shimmerin wi light" suggests twinkling/sparkling effect
- "brightness sharp" suggests intense glow
- "brightness sharp against the gloomy street" suggests light/dark contrast
- "Trees frosted wi light" suggests a silvery glow to the surroundings

- "Lights shaped intae circles and flowers" suggests fantasy-inspired decorations
- "plastic jewellery sets wee lassies love" suggests appealing to children
- "mad rhythm" suggests 'unreal' quality
- "all bleezin wi light" suggests incredibly bright
- "(Amy gazed at them,) eyes shinin" suggests wonder

36. Possible areas for comment include:

Extract:

Reference to main theme of extract e.g. Mother/daughter relationship.

Elsewhere:

- *All that Glisters*
  exploration of relationship between main character and father (who has died), also between main character and mother and auntie
- *Dear Santa*
  exploration of mother daughter relationships (daughter narrates)
- *Zimmerobics*
  exploration of relationship between Miss Knight and her niece Catherine (also with Cheryl from Zimmerobics class)
- *Virtual Pals*
  exploration of the virtual relationship between Siobhan and Irina
- *A Chitterin' Bite*
  exploration between main character and childhood friend, and main character with adult lover

Candidates may choose to answer in **bullet points** in this final question, or write a number of linked statements. There is **no requirement** to write a 'mini essay'.

Up to 2 marks can be achieved for identifying elements of **commonality** as identified in the question.

A further 2 marks can be achieved for **reference to the extract given.**

4 additional marks can be awarded for similar references to **at least one other text/part of the text** by the writer.

<u>In practice this means:</u>

Identification of commonality (2) (e.g. theme, central relationship, importance of setting, use of imagery, development in characterisation, use of personal experience, use of narrative style, or any other key element ...)

From the extract:

1 × relevant reference to technique
1 × appropriate comment

OR 1 × relevant reference to idea
1 × appropriate comment

OR 1 × relevant reference to feature
1 × appropriate comment

OR 1 × relevant reference to text
1 × appropriate comment

(maximum of 2 marks only for discussion of extract)

from at **least one other text/part of the text:**

as above (×2) for **up to 4 marks**

PART C — POETRY — *Mrs Midas* by Carol Ann Duffy

37. 1 mark for reference; 1 mark for comment (×2), up to a maximum of 4 marks.

Possible answers include:

- "glass of wine" suggests leisure time
- "unwind" suggests away from stresses
  NB. Do not accept 'relaxed' as the comment as this is a lift
- "while the vegetables cooked" suggests time to yourself/job done
- "relaxed" suggests taking it easy
- "gently" suggests peaceful/leisurely
- "snapping a twig" suggests something ordinary/harmless/non-threatening

38. 1 mark for reference; 1 mark for comment (×2), up to a maximum of 4 marks.

Possible answers include:

- "(the garden) was long" suggests too far away to see clearly
- "visibility poor" vision impaired by the conditions
- "dark" not enough light to see
- "seems" suggests that she is not sure
- "drink the light of the sky" suggests there is not enough natural light to make out what's happening
- "but that ..." suggests speaker is trying to make sense of what she has seen
- "that twig in his hand was gold" suggests speaker is struggling to make sense of incongruity
- "sat in his palm like a light bulb" suggests speaker is searching for comparisons to explain what she has seen
- "On."/reference to short single word sentence suggests surprise
- "is he putting fairy lights in the tree?"/reference to the question suggests speaker is searching for an explanation

39. 1 mark for reference; 1 mark for comment (×2), up to a maximum of 4 marks.

Possible answers include:

- "He came into the house."/"The doorknobs gleamed."/"He drew the blinds."/reference to short sentences suggests something significant is taking place
- "doorknobs gleamed" suggests unusual/note-worthy shine
- "He sat in that chair like a king" suggests incongruity
- "burnished throne" suggests the chair is transformed/striking
- "strange" suggests out of the ordinary
- "wild" suggests out of control
- "vain" suggests pride/self-important, etc.
- "What in the name of God is going on?"/reference to question suggests an inexplicable/startling event
- "He started to laugh" suggests unsettling reaction

- "Within seconds" suggests things happening rapidly
- "spitting out" suggests violent action
- "corn on the cob into teeth of the rich" suggests rapid transformation of meal into gold
- "toyed" suggests menace/taking pleasure
- "shaking hand" suggests nervousness
- "glass, goblet, golden chalice" disbelief at transformation

40. Possible areas for comment include:

Extract:

Reference to creation of interesting characters in the extract e.g. Mrs Midas – her life being turned upside down by the changes in her husband. Candidates could equally concentrate on changes within Mr Midas.

Elsewhere:

- *War Photographer*
  the character of the war photographer – how he is affected by the things he has seen, and how his work takes him into places which contrast starkly with his home and home country
- *Valentine*
  character displays an 'unusual' take on/attitude to love
- *Havisham*
  character displays ambivalent, and at times hostile, attitude to her ex-lover
- *Anne Hathaway*
  character displays a clear sense of the loss she feels at the memory of her husband
- *Originally*
  Character shows a clear sense of shock brought on by the house-moving. Character struggles with identity

Candidates may choose to answer in **bullet points** in this final question, or write a number of linked statements. There is **no requirement** to write a 'mini essay'.

Up to 2 marks can be achieved for identifying elements of **commonality** as identified in the question.

A further 2 marks can be achieved for **reference to the extract given.**

4 additional marks can be awarded for similar references to **at least one other part of the text** by the writer.

In practice this means:

Identification of commonality (2) (e.g. theme, central relationship, importance of setting, use of imagery, development in characterisation, use of personal experience, use of narrative style, or any other key element ...)

From the extract:

1 × relevant reference to technique
1 × appropriate comment

OR 1 × relevant reference to idea
1 × appropriate comment

OR 1 × relevant reference to feature
1 × appropriate comment

OR 1 × relevant reference to text
1 × appropriate comment

(maximum of 2 marks only for discussion of extract)

from at **least one other text/part of the text:**

as above (×2) for **up to 4 marks**

PART C – POETRY – *Slate* **by Edwin Morgan**

41. 1 mark for reference; 1 mark for comment (×2), up to a maximum of 4 marks.

Possible answers include:

- "saw Lewis laid down" suggests the island of Lewis was placed there as if it was a small, light thing
  OR
- personification of Lewis suggests the deliberate force of the island's formation
- "thunder" suggests noise/danger/drama
- "volcanic fires" suggests the destructive force/ massive elemental force
- "watched long seas plunder faults" suggests the seas were like an army attacking
- "Staffa cooled" suggests the island had to recover from the heat of its formation
- "Drumlins blue as bruises" suggests the hills have been attacked and left hurt/the violent power/ aggression of the formation
- "grated off like nutmegs" suggests the hills were tiny and no match compared to the power of their creator

42. 1 mark for reference; 1 mark for comment (×2), up to a maximum of 4 marks.

Possible answers include:

- "a great glen" suggests the size/magnificence of the glen running across the island
- "a rough back" suggests the island has a tough, resilient protective layer
- "the ages must streak" suggests time will leave a lasting mark
- "surely strike" suggests the island will be attacked as time goes on
- "seldom stroke" suggests the island will rarely be treated kindly
- "raised and shaken" suggests the island will endure despite being treated harshly
- "tens of thousands of rains" highlights the prevalence of rain
- "blizzards" shows the violence of the storms
- "sea-poundings" suggests the sea beat the land
- "shouldered off" suggests the island is able to shrug off these elements/not be beaten by them

43. 1 mark for reference; 1 mark for comment (×2), up to a maximum of 4 marks.

Possible answers include:

- use of two short sentences/contrast of short sentences with previous long sentence highlights the arrival of humans
- positioning of exclamation mark draws our attention to the transition
- "Memory of men!"/"that was to come" suggests the evolving use of the landscape
- "empty hunger"/"threw walls to the sky" personifies the landscape as being eager for something new
- "the sorry glory of a rainbow"/oxymoron highlights the empty and brief beauty of a rainbow compared to the enduring nature of the landscape/the island

- "rainbow" suggests new beginning/hope/new start/ diversity
- "Their heels kicked" suggests impatience for something to happen
- "flint, chalk, slate"/list suggests progression over time

44. Possible areas for comment include:

    Extract: Themes of change, new beginnings, vision of Scotland, violence/brutality of nature, hostile environment.

    Elsewhere:

    - *In the Snack-bar*
      theme of society being uncaring, hostile or challenging environment
    - *Hyena*
      theme of the brutality of nature, hostile/challenging environment
    - *Trio*
      theme of humanism versus religion, idea of hope/ new beginnings
    - *Good Friday*
      theme of religion or social class, challenging environment
    - *Winter*
      theme of death, challenging environment

    Candidates may choose to answer in **bullet points** in this final question, or write a number of linked statements. There is **no requirement** to write a 'mini essay'.

    Up to 2 marks can be achieved for identifying elements of **commonality** as identified in the question.

    A further 2 marks can be achieved for **reference to the extract given.**

    4 additional marks can be awarded for similar references to **at least one other text/part of the text by the writer.**

    <u>In practice this means:</u>

    Identification of commonality (2) (e.g. theme, central relationship, importance of setting, use of imagery, development in characterisation, use of personal experience, use of narrative style, or any other key element ...)

    From the extract:

    1 × relevant reference to technique
    1 × appropriate comment

    OR 1 × relevant reference to idea
    1 × appropriate comment

    OR 1 × relevant reference to feature
    1 × appropriate comment

    OR 1 × relevant reference to text
    1 × appropriate comment

    (maximum of 2 marks only for discussion of extract)

    from at **least one other text/part of the text:**

    as above (× 2) for up to **4 marks**

PART C — POETRY — *Memorial* by Norman MacCaig

45. 1 mark for each point, up to a maximum of 2 marks.

    Possible answers include:

    - he no longer feels enjoyment
    - her death is with him at all times in all places

- her death interrupts everything
- her death restricts his ability to communicate
- he cannot get close to other people/another person
- she still seems to influence him
- he feels isolated/apart from her

46. 1 mark for reference; 1 mark for comment (×2), up to a maximum of 4 marks.

    Possible answers include:

    - repetition of "Everywhere" emphasises omnipresence of her death
    - repetition of "no" emphasises there is no escape from the fact of her death
    - contrast of "silence" and "carousel" suggests the removal of joy from his life
    - "it's a web" feels restricted or trapped
    - "How can my hand clasp ..." suggests that loved one is irreplaceable
    - reference to question suggests he can't find answers/ no closure
    - "Thick (death)" suggests the heavy weight of her death enveloping him
    - "intolerable" hard to bear
    - "distance" suggests isolation/loneliness following death, etc.

47. 1 mark for reference; 1 mark for comment (×2), up to a maximum of 4 marks.

    Possible answers include:

    - "She grieves for my grief" she appears to share his emotions/emotional reactions
    - "she tells me" she still communicates with him
    - "(her dying) shapes my mind" continued influence
    - "But I hear" suggests continued presence
    - use of present tense suggests continued closeness
    - repetition of words suggests her voice still seems to be there

48. 1 mark for reference; 1 mark for comment.

    Possible answers include:

    - expression from ending
    - linked reference/idea from elsewhere
      NB The linked reference may be to the poem as a whole
    - "elegy" relates to the form of the poem
    - "walking" refers back to idea of "Everywhere I go"
    - "masterpiece" refers back to idea of "carved more gently"
    - "true fiction" refers back to idea of "black words"
    - "ugliness of death" refers back to idea of "thick death"/death is mentioned many times in the poem
    - "I am her sad music" refers back to idea of "sound of soundlessness" etc

49. Possible areas for comment include:

    Extract:

    Reference to use of language exploring experiences of death and loss.

Elsewhere:

- *Basking Shark*
  description of the encounter with the shark, and how it caused the poet to think/reflect on how he viewed man/nature, etc.

- *Visiting Hour*
  language reflects the difficulty of dealing with feelings/making sense of highly charged emotional experience

- *Assisi*
  language reflects important discoveries about how society/the church treats disabled/vulnerable/poor people

- *Aunt Julia*
  language concentrates on discovery of the importance of the past/people from the past/people who are no longer with us. Importance of/remoteness of other cultures

- *Sounds of the day*
  word choice/imagery reflects the lasting effects/impact of the parting.

Candidates may choose to answer in **bullet points** in this final question, or write a number of linked statements. There is **no requirement** to write a 'mini essay'.

Up to 2 marks can be achieved for identifying elements of **commonality** as identified in the question.

A further 2 marks can be achieved for **reference to the extract given.**

4 additional marks can be awarded for similar references to **at least one other part of the text** by the writer.

In practice this means:

Identification of commonality (2) (e.g. theme, central relationship, importance of setting, use of imagery, development in characterisation, use of personal experience, use of narrative style, or any other key element …)

From the extract:

1 × relevant reference to technique
1 × appropriate comment

OR 1 × relevant reference to idea
1 × appropriate comment

OR 1 × relevant reference to feature
1 × appropriate comment

OR 1 × relevant reference to text
1 × appropriate comment

(maximum of 2 marks only for discussion of extract)

from at **least one other text/part of the text:**

as above (×2) for **up to 4 marks**

PART C — POETRY — *Gap Year* by Jackie Kay

50. 1 mark for reference; 1 mark for comment.

    Possible answers include:

    - "I'd stare" suggests intense interest
    - "for days"/"weeks" suggests interest so great it was maintained over a period of time

- "willing you" suggests sense of anticipation
- "hardly able to believe" suggests can't comprehend the enormity of the event
- "real baby" suggests the reality is momentous

51. 1 mark for reference; 1 mark for comment (×2), up to a maximum of 4 marks.

    Possible answers include:

    - "I'd feel the mound" suggests physical closeness
    - "foot against my heart" suggests extreme closeness
    - "I imagined I felt you laugh" suggests absorption in the experience
    - "I'd play you … (music)" suggests a sense of nurture
    - "I'd talk to you" suggests communication
    - "my close stranger" suggests early intimacy
    - "Tumshie" suggests playful nickname
    - "ask when you were coming to meet me" suggests excitement/anticipation

52. (a) 1 mark for reference; 1 mark for comment (×2), up to a maximum of 4 marks.

    Possible answers include:

    - "stare at your bed" indicates she is missing her son
    - "Your handsome face" indicates a sense of pride
    - repetition of "away" suggests isolation/distance between them
    - the many references to different places "Costa Rica … Machu Picchu", etc. indicates wonderment at the scale of the trip
    - "I follow your trails" indicates absorption
    - the use of "from … to" structure indicates admiration for the distance travelled
    - references to time "Now … then … yesterday" indicate admiration for the length of the trip
    - references to "photograph/web cam" indicate pride that the trip is being documented
    - "your face is grainy, blurry" reiterates the distance between them

    (b) 1 mark for reference; 1 mark for comment.

    Possible answers include:

    - "Have you considered" indicates realism/lack of romance/implied criticism of mother
    - "altitude sickness" indicates warning of potential danger
    - "Christ" indicates exasperation/disapproval
    - "sixteen thousand feet above sea level" reiterates remoteness/danger/hostile environment

53. Possible areas for comment include:

    Extract:

    Reference to bedroom at home or a destination (Costa Rica, Peru, Bolivia) – comment might include mention of themes of isolation, loss, separation, growing up, family relationships, identity, or could focus on character and/or character relationships.

Elsewhere:

- *Keeping Orchids*
  settings of home and train station leading to comments on – family relationships, sense of identity, characters of mother and daughter, etc.

- *Lucozade*
  hospital setting leading to comments on – family relationships, sense of identity, loss, separation, etc.

- *My grandmother's Houses*
  settings of old home, new home, cleaning house leading to comments on – family relationships, identity, etc.

- *Bed*
  hospital setting leading to comments on – family relationships, isolation, separation, etc.

Candidates may choose to answer in **bullet points** in this final question, or write a number of linked statements. There is **no requirement** to write a 'mini essay'.

Up to 2 marks can be achieved for identifying elements of commonality as requested in the question.

A further 2 marks can be achieved for **reference to the extract given.**

4 additional marks can be awarded for similar references to **at least one other part of the text.**

In practice this means:

Identification of commonality (2) (e.g. theme, central relationship, importance of setting, use of imagery, development in characterisation, use of personal experience, use of narrative style or any other key element ...)

From the extract:

1 × relevant reference to technique **1** × appropriate comment

OR 1 × relevant reference to idea 1 × appropriate comment

OR 1 × relevant reference to feature 1 × appropriate comment

OR 1 × relevant reference to text 1 × appropriate comment

(maximum of 2 marks only for discussion of extract)

from at **least one other part of the text:**

as above (×2) for **up to 4 marks**

SECTION 2 – CRITICAL ESSAY

Please see the assessment criteria for the Critical Essay on page 127.

NATIONAL 5 ENGLISH 2019

READING FOR UNDERSTANDING, ANALYSIS AND EVALUATION

1. Any two points for 1 mark each.

   Glosses of:
   - "follow in the footsteps of Diana Ross and Whitney Houston" e.g. she was a great (female) singer/star too
   - "belt out" e.g. give a powerful delivery
   - "the voice of Elsa"/"the most successful animated film …" e.g. she was the singer of the hit film/song
   - "ubiquitous" e.g. the song was heard everywhere (accept e.g. "was well known")
   - "Oscar-winning" e.g. the song was critically acclaimed
   - "more than three million copies sold" e.g. the song was (very) popular/profitable
   - "(more than passing) acquaintance" e.g. she has (good) experience "with anthems" e.g. of important/highly-regarded songs

2. 1 mark for reference; 1 mark for comment.
   - "stratospheric" e.g. suggests signal/immense/far-reaching/heightened achievement/out of this world
   - "(takings of more than) £800 million" OR "it's No 5 in the all-time list of highest-grossing films" OR uses statistics e.g. to show that the film has made a great deal of money
   - uses parenthesis to include (significant) statistics/evidence
   - "has elevated her" e.g. she has achieved greater prominence
   - "into a new league" e.g. into a different (superior) context

3. Any five points.

   Glosses of:
   - "she has clearly been reprimanded" e.g. they have a system of discipline/control
   - "by the Disney suits" e.g. they are conventionally dressed (ie reference to appearance)
   - "by the Disney suits" e.g. conservative/corporate/faceless (i.e. reference to attitude/mindset)
   - "Apparently I spoke out of turn" e.g. they disliked dissent
   - "Disney doesn't have sequels, (so it would be a first if there was one)" e.g. they don't (usually) produce follow-up films
   - "stage show" OR "six-minute short" OR "new song" indicates e.g. (commercial) versatility
   - "(much) mooted" e.g. Disney is the centre of speculation
   - "the Disney people keep things close to their chests" OR "tight-lipped" e.g. they are secretive/they say little
   - "happy to milk the commercial opportunities" OR "enjoyed a mighty bump" e.g. they take pleasure in exploiting/maximising the financial gain

4. 1 mark for reference; 1 mark for comment (×2).
   - "There to be shot at" e.g. suggests people's readiness to denigrate OR (image of) "shot at" illustrates e.g. the critics' aggression/hostility/targeting
   - "criticised" e.g. indicates open to negative comment
   - "failing to hit a high note" e.g. suggest harshness of criticism
   - parenthetical insertion (of "singing in sub-zero temperatures") e.g. serves to highlight the point
   - substance of "sub-zero temperatures" e.g. adverse conditions
   - "still some who noticed the odd flat note" e.g. suggests (excessive) vigilance of audience/inability to please everyone
   - "The unnerving" e.g. it is scary
   - "proximity" e.g. the footballers are close
   - "of several dozen" e.g. there are many of them
   - "hulking (American footballers)" OR "huge" e.g. they are very big/intimidating
   - "strong presence (these athletes have)" e.g. they have an aura/charisma
   - "you're this one woman, singing on her own" e.g. she was alone/an outnumbered female
   - "(they're so …) daunting" e.g. (the men are) intimidating
   - use of ellipsis suggests she wants to be precise in her own comments/provides a dramatic pause/emphasises "daunting"

5. Any one pair OR two correct selections covering different directions.
   - "One woman" looks back to "one woman" OR "on her own" OR the idea of isolation
   - "squad of men" looks back to "several dozen hulking" OR "huge" OR "American footballers" OR the idea of male physical presence
   - "Frozen" looks forward to "Disney animation"
   - "a feminist breakthrough" looks forward to (idea of) "The first … to be directed … by a woman" OR "love … between two sisters" OR "not because some Prince Charming is saving the day"
   - "One woman opposite a squad of men" (accept paraphrase) looks back to the isolation of Idina Menzel
   - information before colon looks back information after colon looks forward

6. 1 mark for reference; 1 mark for comment (×2).
   - "heroine" e.g. strength of character
   - "subtle" e.g. not straightforward
   - "conflicted" e.g. has contradictory emotions/internal battles/complications
   - "sorceress" e.g. supernatural
   - "struggling to control her powers" e.g. has difficulties with her abilities
   - "she keeps [Anna] at a distance" e.g. deliberately remote
   - "for fear of turning her into a popsicle" e.g. she wields (potentially harmful) power

- "(grandiose) sulks" e.g. is (spectacularly) moody
- "emo (princess)" e.g. alternative/sensitive/of dark mind or appearance/saturnine
- "(definitely) complicated" e.g. (undeniably) complex
- "not stereotypes" e.g. not predictable/what is conventionally expected

7.
- her sister's company (beautifully) encapsulated key ideas of the films
- **OR** Travolta's error heightened her profile
- **OR** the song was up for (and won) an (top) award — "Oscar" may be lifted and she got to sing it

8. It is possible to gain full marks through examination of one linguistic aspect.

Sentence structure:
- long compared to short sentences **OR** appropriate contrasting references shows complexity compared simplicity

Tone:
- appropriate contrasting references e.g. "several zeitgeist-y things across different generations"/"people who are trying to find themselves" compared with "one more (burning) question"/"No I do not!" shows formality/seriousness compared to lightness/humour/vehemence

Word choice:
- "zeitgeist-y" **OR** "resonate" compared to "Does she have her own Elsa dress" shows the difference between difficulty and simplicity
- "proud" and "much to learn" exhibits the difference between self-esteem and humility
- "Rent to Wicked" **OR** "Glee to Frozen" illustrates then and now
- "Frozen" and "burning". Comment must show understanding these are antonyms
- "certainly aware" and "I have as much to learn myself". Comment must show understanding these are antonymous

9. *Any five from:*

Reference to	Glossed by (e.g.)
"I spoke out of turn"	She can be forthright/impulsive
"I'd have to play Elsa's mother, probably" or "she laughs"	She has a (self-deprecating) sense of humour
"she sounds slightly disappointed"	She likes to be the star/centre of attention/is self-centred
Despite criticisms	She shows persistence
"they're ... daunting"	She can be intimidated
"not because some Prince Charming is saving the day"	She is assertive/feminist (accept slang)
"It was Cara whom Menzel took as her date"	She is close to/fond of her sister/caring
"wincingly"	She is modest/embarrassed by her sister's admiration

Reference to	Glossed by (e.g.)
"she ... recognises ... Travolta's slip"	She is perceptive/realistic
"her conversation is a mix of Broadway-speak"	She can be/is shrewd enough to adapt to her environment/use platitudes
"battled-hardened"	She is tough/resilient
"ambition"	She has aspirations
"aware of the value of appearing"	She is shrewd/pragmatic
"I'm proud of that"	She relishes fans' identification with her
"I have as much to learn myself"	She is modest/self-aware
"I don't look that good as a blonde"	She is modest NB please don't credit 'modest' twice
"she'd also quite enjoy ruling over her own wintry kingdom"	She enjoys power/dominance/prominence

CRITICAL READING

SECTION 1 – SCOTTISH TEXT

PART A – DRAMA – *Bold Girls* by Rona Munro

1. Any four points for 1 mark each.

Possible answers include:
- Marie reflects on her relationship with Michael (her deceased husband)
- Marie admits she knew more about what was going on than she ever spoke about at the time
- Marie states that Cassie is justified in her critical comments
- Marie admits she recognised who Deirdre was on their first meeting
- Marie says she tried to look after Michael when he was upset
- Deirdre promises to return all the money but Marie says it isn't important
- Marie says she will give the money back to Cassie
- Deirdre says she's going home/Marie stops her
- Marie admits that Michael was Deirdre's father/and that they look similar
- Marie offers Deirdre some breakfast
- Marie tells Deirdre about how she likes to feed the birds/and encourages her to join in

2. 1 mark for reference; 1 mark for comment (×2), for a maximum of 4 marks.

Possible answers include:
- 'It wasn't that I lied' suggests she is trying to make excuses
- 'all the truth' suggests she knew more than she was admitting
- 'You'd be crazy ...' suggests she is getting emotional
- '... he'd have to change'/'Maybe he'd sooner leave.' suggests her uncertainty of how he might react
- 'I didn't want him to leave' suggests fear of losing him

- Repetition of ('I loved him.')/'I loved him.' suggests her commitment to Michael
- '... even now' suggests lasting feelings
- '... I'm just a mug.' suggests honesty/frankness
- 'Cassie was right.' suggests awareness
- 'I knew who you were ...' suggests she can cope with the truth
- 'What good would ... do you?'/rhetorical question suggests she seeks validation from Deirdre
- Uses a series of 3 rhetorical questions in a row suggests Marie is trying to justify her thinking at the time
- Series of sentences starting with personal pronoun 'I' suggests self-reflection
- Use of (several) short sentences towards the end of her speech suggests moment of realisation/honesty/confession
- 'What age are you?' suggests she is seeking confirmation

3. 1 mark for example of dialogue, 1 mark for comment; 1 mark for example of stage direction, 1 mark for comment, for a maximum of 4 marks.

Possible answers include:

Dialogue

- 'It doesn't matter' lets her off with repaying the missing £5
- 'You're shivering' shows concern for her physical comfort
- 'You can't go out like that.' tries to stop her being uncomfortable/cold
- '... he never told me.' reassures Deirdre that she hadn't been deliberately ignoring her existence
- 'You've got his eyes.' admits the physical similarity to Michael
- '... I'll get the breakfast started ...' looks after Deirdre's wellbeing
- 'You can give me a hand if you like' invites Deirdre to join in
- 'You make crumbs of that.' allows Deirdre to join in with feeding the birds (which is one of Marie's favourite activities)

Stage directions

- '(*she shakes her head*)' is generous in saying that Deirdre's repayment will benefit Cassie
- '*They look at each other for a minute*' moment of realisation/tenderness
- '(*She moves back to the kitchen and starts getting out food*)' shows Marie is going to make her a meal
- '(*Handing her a loaf*)' involves Deirdre in the preparation
- '*Lights fade to Black-out*' leaves an optimistic (final) stage picture for the future relationship of Marie and Deirdre

4. *Possible areas for comment include:*

Extract:

Marie and Deirdre may form a 'mother/daughter' relationship in the future. They seem to have

reconciled their differences by the end of the play. The tension between them has lessened and there is the acknowledgement that Deirdre is Michael's daughter. The play ends with them involved together in a domestic task (preparing breakfast) which they haven't shared together before this point.

Marie's relationship with Michael — she loved him/venerated him/accepted his faults/was terrified of losing him.

Elsewhere:

Marie's relationship with Michael — she defends/idolises him throughout the play.

Presentation of males in families — often absent or the source of conflict. Michael (husband/father), Joe (husband/father), and Sean (brother/son).

Marie and her children (Michael Junior and Brendan) — Marie puts her children first and wants the best for them. Sometimes, Cassie (Marie's best friend) helps with their domestic routine as she frequently 'pops' round. Marie is house-proud and tries to make a happy home for her children (despite not having much money).

Deirdre and her biological mother are not close — Deirdre has been the victim of domestic abuse at the hands of her mother's boyfriend. Her mother seems aware of this but doesn't stop this from happening.

Nora and Cassie argue at many points of the play as they have different 'standards' about dress and behaviour. Nora thinks that Cassie is too 'flamboyant' and too 'loud'. However, they support each other with domestic hardships. The source of their arguing is the different opinions they hold about Sean (Nora's dead husband) and Joe (Cassie's incarcerated husband). They both view these men in extremely opposite ways. Cassie adored her father whilst Nora says he was often violent. Nora thinks Joe is an 'ideal husband' — Cassie doesn't.

Candidates may choose to answer in bullet points in this final question, or write a number of linked statements. There is no requirement to write a 'mini essay'.

Up to 2 marks can be achieved for identifying elements of **commonality** as identified in the question.

A further 2 marks can be achieved for **reference to the extract given.**

4 additional marks can be awarded for similar references to **at least one other part of the text** by the writer.

In practice this means:

Identification of commonality (2) (e.g. theme, central relationship, importance of setting, use of imagery, development in characterisation, use of personal experience, use of narrative style, or any other key element ...)

From the extract:

1 relevant reference to technique; 1 appropriate comment

OR 1 relevant reference to idea; 1 appropriate comment

OR 1 relevant reference to feature; 1 appropriate comment

OR 1 relevant reference to text; 1 appropriate comment

(maximum of 2 marks only for discussion of extract)

from at **least one other part of the text:**

as above (×2) for **up to 4 marks**

PART A — DRAMA — *Sailmaker* by Alan Spence

5. 1 mark for reference; 1 mark for comment (×2), for a maximum of 4 marks.

Possible answers include:

- 'singing'/'sings'/Alec is singing in the house suggests he is excited to go
- Knows the words of the songs (by heart) suggests his dedication
- 'Give me oil'/'keep me burning'/'I pray'/'Halleluja' suggests a desire to keep going/be involved/shows it is important to Alec
- Exclamation mark (line 5) suggests strength of feeling
- 'religious fanatic' suggests devotion
- Reference to or examples of number of evenings/ accumulation of groups suggests the depth of involvement/amount of time he invests
- 'too young' suggests the extraordinary level of interest
- He was invited by the minister suggests he has been identified as particularly interested
- 'top in the bible exam'/'Top equal.' suggests he is dedicated

6. 1 mark for reference; 1 mark for comment (×2), for a maximum of 4 marks.

Possible answers include:

- 'keeps ye aff the streets' suggests Davie is pleased Alec is safe/has an interest in something
- 'Mind yer heid …' shows Davie is making fun of Alec/ is proud of Alec
- Negative comments about the mirror/'really stupid'/'annoyin' suggest Alec is critical of Davie (for putting up with the broken mirror)
- 'a big crack down the middle'/'two halfs don't sit right' suggests (symbolically) the underlying issues between them
- 'Canny get a good look at yerself.' suggests that Alec is frustrated by Davie's lack of self-awareness
- 'Ach away ye go!' suggests (mock) exasperation
- Argument about the missing bible/'Try lookin …'/ 'Where?' suggests a typical parent/child disagreement

7. 1 mark for reference; 1 mark for comment (×2), for a maximum of 4 marks.

Possible answers include:

- Davie has read/enjoyed the book/'Good book that'/'Ah read it …' suggests his intelligence/interest in literature
- 'ah was in the Boy's Brigade' suggests as a child he was similar to Alec/was previously religious/positive memories
- 'made me want to be a missionary' suggests his once adventurous/ambitious side/was very serious about religion at one time
- 'Just … drifted away fae it' suggests he did not pursue his interests/gave up on his dreams
- Use of ellipsis suggests his struggle to articulate why he didn't follow his dreams

- 'darkest Govan' suggests his self-deprecating nature/ sense of humour
- (Repeats) 'First Prize' suggests he is proud of his son
- Positive references to his (dead) wife suggests his fondness for her/sense of sadness at his loss/lack of self belief
- 'wurnae the same opportunities' suggests Davie is making excuses for himself/passive response to his circumstances/sense of unfairness
- Reference to/example of colloquial language **or** Scots reflects his origins/place of birth
- Encouragement of Alec's education shows that he believes in his son/wants a better life for Alec/knows that education is a vehicle for escaping poverty
- 'Will your anchor hold' suggests Davie has not always coped with the difficulties
- 'storms of life'/'wings of strife' suggests Davie has endured some difficult experiences
- Remembers the lyrics of the song suggests it was once important to him

8. *Possible areas for comment include:*

Extract:

'keeps ye aff the streets' suggests Davie feels that where they live can have negative elements.

Davie encourages Alec's interest in religion and education as he sees them as positive influences and opportunities for people to escape from poverty. He is ambitious for Alec to have a more comfortable life where he can be successful and well rewarded for his intelligence.

Elsewhere:

References to the setting in Govan/Glasgow and the bleak surroundings including the decline of the shipbuilding industry and its impact on the community.

References to a traditional Scottish working class background where men worked in trades and were patriarchs of their families. This impacts on Davie as he struggles to talk about his issues with anyone and then loses his status with his declining employment.

Some people (e.g. Ian) viewing middle classes with suspicion/ridicule.

Alec's character makes the journey from working class to middle class using education as he progresses to a different school and then university.

Alec's subsequent distance from his family as he changes with his education and changing social circle, where he learns about and considers different lifestyles (e.g. vegetarianism, Buddhism) which they find alienating/ ridiculous.

Ian and Billy are shown as contrasting examples to Alec where education is not valued and following tradition is important, e.g. liking the same football team, going into the same trade.

References to other people who have escaped (or attempted to escape) poverty through other methods, e.g. sport, emigration. As well as characters struggling with alcoholism, gambling, debt, etc.

The inclusion of the quotations from the book 'The British Working Man' which provides both accuracy and irony.

Candidates may choose to answer in bullet points in this final question, or write a number of linked statements. There is no requirement to write a 'mini essay'.

Up to 2 marks can be achieved for identifying elements of **commonality** as identified in the question.

A further 2 marks can be achieved for **reference to the extract given.**

4 additional marks can be awarded for similar references to **at least one other part of the text** by the writer.

<u>In practice this means:</u>

Identification of commonality (2) (e.g. theme, central relationship, importance of setting, use of imagery, development in characterisation, use of personal experience, use of narrative style, or any other key element …)

From the extract:

1 relevant reference to technique; 1 appropriate comment

OR 1 relevant reference to idea; 1 appropriate comment

OR 1 relevant reference to feature; 1 appropriate comment

OR 1 relevant reference to text; 1 appropriate comment

(maximum of 2 marks only for discussion of extract)

from at **least one other part of the text:**

as above (×2) for **up to 4 marks**

PART A — DRAMA — *Tally's Blood* by Ann Marie Di Mambro

9. Any two for 1 mark each.

Possible answers include:

- They put in more effort (than others)/long hours
  NB: accept 'work' only with qualifying comment

- They create their own employment/are self-employed

- They don't replace local workers/Scottish workers
  NB: Do not accept 'jobs' as it is a lift

- They keep to themselves/have their own community

- They contribute to the economy/can support themselves/do not expect handouts

- They are well behaved/follow the rules

10. Any two for 1 mark each.

- Massimo wants to leave/return to Italy while it is possible/before something bad happens

- Rosinella wants to stay/feels that they have too much to lose by leaving

- Massimo is afraid/worried/concerned/anxious

- Rosinella feels that because he is popular/admired/accepted by the community nothing negative will happen

11. 1 mark for reference; 1 mark for comment (×2), for a maximum of 4 marks.

Possible answers include:

- 'since I was a wee boy' suggests nostalgia/bittersweet

- List of three or specific examples ('school', 'brother was born', 'mammy's buried') suggests he has a real sense of belonging to Scotland

- '(always thought I was) lucky' suggests he (previously) felt fortunate

- 'two countries' suggests he felt a kinship with Italy and Scotland

- Use of/example of the past tense suggests sadness/sense of being misguided

- 'nowhere'/anti-climax suggests sense of loss/isolation/disappointment

- Short sentences suggest his (building) frustration/despair

12. 1 mark for reference; 1 mark for comment (×2), for a maximum of 4 marks.

Possible answers include:

- They are playfully re-enacting actions of war which is the wider concern of the adults

- 'shooting sounds getting louder' suggests the sense of rising tension

- Repeated use of sound/impact of 'Pee-aiow' echoes the unwelcome intrusion of war in their lives

- Lucia (Italy) and Hughie (Scotland) represent the different nationalities at war/sides of the conflict which is the main concern of the extract

- 'I don't like this'/'I don't like it' suggests the negative impact of war on the people affected

- '*threatened*'/'*cowering*' suggests the fear that other people, e.g. Massimo, also experience

- '*kicks Hughie on the shin*' suggests (on a smaller scale) the violence (which is an aspect of war)

- '*he continues to circle her*'/'Beat it, Hughie Devlin!' suggests actions allude to future romantic relationship/flirtatious

  NB be aware of identification or description of the idea of microcosm as an acceptable answer.

13. *Possible areas for comment include:*

Extract:

Massimo is concerned about the outbreak of war and the negative impact that it will have on them.

Rosinella is naive and believes that the war won't affect them as 'ordinary working people' or Massimo because he is respected in the community.

The younger characters have only a childish understanding of war.

Massimo feels conflicted between his love of Italy and his love of Scotland because the two countries will be on either side of the war.

Elsewhere:

Franco signs up to the army believing it will give him freedom from his family but he dies in war.

Massimo's shop is later attacked by a mob because he is Italian.

Massimo and his father are arrested and then deported and separated from each other as prisoners of war.

Massimo's monologue details the suffering that Italians faced while they were prisoners.

Massimo's father is killed at war when the ship he is on sinks.

The negative impact on the women who are left behind, e.g. Bridget, Rosinella and Lucia.

The impact of the war on Italy where much of the country was bombed and Massimo's family have suffered losses.

The impact on the Pedreschi family business as they are affected by rationing and hostility from the Scottish community.

Rosinella is left feeling bitter about the impact of the war years later refusing to get over the way Italians treated them.

Candidates may choose to answer in bullet points in this final question, or write a number of linked statements. There is no requirement to write a 'mini essay'.

Up to 2 marks can be achieved for identifying elements of **commonality** as identified in the question.

A further 2 marks can be achieved for **reference to the extract given**.

4 additional marks can be awarded for similar references to **at least one other part of the text** by the writer.

<u>In practice this means:</u>

Identification of commonality (2) (e.g. theme, central relationship, importance of setting, use of imagery, development in characterisation, use of personal experience, use of narrative style, or any other key element ...)

From the extract:

1 relevant reference to technique; 1 appropriate comment

OR 1 relevant reference to idea; 1 appropriate comment

OR 1 relevant reference to feature; 1 appropriate comment

OR 1 relevant reference to text; 1 appropriate comment

(maximum of 2 marks only for discussion of extract)

from **at least one other part of the text:**

as above (×2) for **up to 4 marks**

PART B – PROSE – *The Cone-Gatherers* by Robin Jenkins

14. 1 mark for reference; 1 mark for comment (×2), for a maximum of 4 marks.

Possible answers include:

- 'consummate' suggests expert/talented/accomplished
- 'confidence' suggests self-assured/knew he was good at it
- 'grace' suggests elegance/beauty/poise
- 'inner night' suggests darkness/difficulty of the task
- 'Not once ... was he at a loss' suggests he always knew what to do/never faltered
- 'all the long way down' suggests it was a tall tree
- 'find holds by instinct' suggests felt at one with nature/was led by intuition/unconsciously knew what to do
- 'patiently guided his brother's feet' suggests was able to help Neil at the same time
- 'superiority as a climber' suggests this is an area of strength

15. 1 mark for reference; 1 mark for comment (×2), for a maximum of two marks

Possible answers include:

- 'hurrying to keep close behind' suggests he struggled to keep up with his brother
- '(often) stumbled'/'he would trip over it' suggests he (frequently) fell

- 'Gone were the balance and sureness' suggests he no longer felt at ease
- 'mishaps'/'scrambled' suggests undignified/struggle/lack of poise
- 'anxious' suggests worried
- 'hindrance' suggests he was holding his brother back

16. (a) 1 mark for reference; 1 mark for comment.

Possible answers include:

Duror:

- 'waiting for them outside their hut' suggests he was prepared to intrude on their privacy/wanted to make them feel uncomfortable
- 'His rage'/'(quiet but) intimidating' suggests he was angry/menacing/had a calm but frightening fury
- 'gun raised (once or twice to emphasise)/threats' suggests he tried to scare them/hinted at his potential for (deadly) violence

(b) 1 mark for reference; 1 mark for comment.

Possible answers include:

Neil:

- 'Neil had said little in reply' suggests he kept calm/did not argue back
- 'faced up to the gun raised' suggests he did not show any fear/showed he was prepared to stand up for himself (and his brother)

(c) 1 mark for reference; 1 mark for comment.

Possible answers include:

Calum:

- 'demoralised (as always by hatred)' suggests he was saddened by the argument/he was deflated by Duror being annoyed with them/struggled to cope with disagreements
- 'cowered (against the hut)' suggests his fear/panic
- 'hiding (his face)' suggests he will not stand up to his opponent/childlike response

17. *Possible areas for comment include:*

Extract:

The brothers rely on each other, e.g. Calum helps Neil in the trees, but Neil helps Calum on the ground.

Neil tries to guide Calum to understand how the world works, e.g. not setting rabbits free from traps.

Calum doesn't always understand Neil, e.g. the importance of swearing on the life of a woman who is already dead that he can't remember.

Neil gets frustrated at Calum, e.g. when he releases the rabbits which he knows will lead to difficulties with Duror.

Calum is endlessly loving towards Neil, e.g. doesn't complain when he stands on his hand.

Calum doesn't want to disappoint Neil, e.g. tries to keep up with him on the ground.

Elsewhere:

Neil takes on the protective role/they have a parent-child dynamic, e.g. Neil worries about what would happen to Calum without him.

Neil has to tend to practical matters such as clothing, ordering food.

Mr. Tulloch tells Neil that 'no man on earth has ever looked after his brother so well'.

Neil tries to get Calum the best possible spot on the deer drive/has to be strict with him about the deer drive etc.

Calum wants to do what he can for Neil, e.g. buy him a present in Lendrick, carves him animals. Neil has made sacrifices to look after Calum, e.g. did not marry which causes him to feel sad/lonely.

Neil recognises Calum's good nature, e.g. 'better and wiser than any of them'.

Neil defends Calum, e.g. 'my brother's the shape God made him'.

Neil gets frustrated with Calum, e.g. 'are you such a child you're going to cry …'.

Neil feels shame whenever he is embarrassed by or angry with Calum, e.g. when Calum wants to apologise for the deer drive.

There are areas of disagreement, e.g. Calum does not want to go into the beach hut because he knows they are not supposed to but Neil is determined to do it/they differ in their beliefs about God and heaven.

Candidates may choose to answer in bullet points in this final question, or write a number of linked statements. There is no requirement to write a 'mini essay'.

Up to 2 marks can be achieved for identifying elements of **commonality** as identified in the question.

A further 2 marks can be achieved for **reference to the extract given.**

4 additional marks can be awarded for similar references to **at least one other part of the text** by the writer.

<u>In practice this means:</u>

Identification of commonality (2) (e.g. theme, central relationship, importance of setting, use of imagery, development in characterisation, use of personal experience, use of narrative style, or any other key element …)

From the extract:

1 relevant reference to technique; 1 appropriate comment

OR 1 relevant reference to idea; 1 appropriate comment

OR 1 relevant reference to feature; 1 appropriate comment

OR 1 relevant reference to text; 1 appropriate comment

(maximum of 2 marks only for discussion of extract)

from at **least one other part of the text:**

as above (×2) for **up to 4 marks**

PART B — PROSE — *The Testament of Gideon Mack* by James Robertson

18. 1 mark for reference; 1 mark for comment (×2), for a maximum of 4 marks.

Possible answers include:

- 'We stared at him' suggests what he is saying is unusual
- 'incomprehension' suggests they cannot understand what is going on
- 'tiny (thrilling) hope' suggests the chance is very slim
- 'joke' suggests it cannot be real

- 'there had never been any question of it being allowed in the manse' suggests this is an extreme turnaround
- 'like alcohol' suggests it is a sin
- 'a distillation of all the vices he most detested' suggests he would clearly never have had it in the house before
- '(he associated it with) America, in his mind the wellspring of those selfsame vices' suggests the reason why he had hated it so much before
- repetition of/word choice of 'vices' emphasises how badly he had previously regarded television
- 'and now' suggests a complete change of heart
- 'here he was' suggests this was a remarkable event
- 'monster' suggests a horrific thing, not to be admitted
- contrast/alliteration of 'monster' and 'manse' emphasises how unlikely this is

19. Any two for 1 mark each.

Possible answers include:

- 'we must move with the times', e.g. he recognises things are changing and wants to be part of that
- 'see the news', e.g. he wants the visual news, rather than only getting audio on the radio
- 'educational programmes', e.g. there are good resources to help with Gideon's learning
- 'major sporting events', e.g. it's an opportunity to watch sports he cannot attend in person

20. 1 mark for reference; 1 mark for comment (×2), for a maximum of 4 marks.

Possible answers include:

- 'admitted' suggests a reluctance
- 'suppressed horror' suggests he is trying to control his true feelings
- 'corrosive' suggests he thinks it is damaging
- 'glowered' suggests distaste
- 'guest' suggests this is temporary
- '(extremely) doubtful character' suggests distrust
- 'it was only a matter of time' suggests he is waiting for an inevitable slip-up
- 'outrageously' suggests extremity of expectation
- 'offensive' suggests dislike
- 'it did'/'it showed England winning the world cup' suggests his fears were realised
- 'it had also … highest level' suggests more positive feelings here as this is welcome
- 'he had let the beast in' suggests he feels responsible/guilt
- 'beast' suggests he thinks of it as a monster
- 'an admission of error' suggests his pride is at stake
- 'gradually' suggests he is starting to relent
- 'rules' suggests he likes to be in control of it
- 'relaxed' suggests he is easing off a bit/getting used to it

21. One mark for each point.

    Possible answers include:

    - 'One was watching American trash', e.g. he isn't allowed to view programmes from the US that Gideon's father considers to be rubbish but that Gideon loves
    - 'Sunday', e.g. the Sabbath was sacred to Gideon's father so the television could not be watched that day

22. *Possible areas for comment include:*

    Extract:

    Gideon and his mother are shocked at Gideon's father bringing television into the home. This suggests they see his behaviour as hypocritical.

    Gideon and his mother don't dare question Gideon's father's decisions. This shows how domineering he is.

    Gideon's mother shows 'incomprehension,' and has not been consulted about the television. This suggests that Gideon's father makes all the decisions.

    Elsewhere:

    Gideon's relationship with his father

    Gideon's father is very strict/domineering/physically domineering.

    Gideon's father imposes strict religious regime on Gideon.

    Gideon feels his father is disappointed in him. Gideon pretends to have religious faith in order to please him. This deception leads to other deceptions for Gideon.

    No real connection with father; however, Gideon ironically becomes a Minister like his father.

    Gideon's relationship with his mother

    No real bond with mother.

    Gideon's mother is able to explain some of Gideon's father's motivation and fears to Gideon.

    Relationship worsens when Gideon's mother is in nursing home and doesn't recognise Gideon.

    Gideon's relationship with his wife

    Gideon has problematic relationship with his wife. Admits he has had long-term relationship with Elsie Moffat.

    Elsewhere:

    The past is represented by, e.g. local history; the standing stones; folklore; superstition; stories within stories; traditional values; the church; the characterisation of Gideon's father.

    The future is represented by, e.g. technology; modern culture; awareness of the wider country/world; changing attitudes to relationships, religion etc; the role of the publisher in the narrative; characters' reluctance to believe the more supernatural elements of the story; the characterisation of Catherine Craigie and of Gideon himself.

    Candidates may choose to discuss the continuum and evolution from past to present as the novel has a foot in both camps throughout as the lists above co-exist.

    Candidates may also choose to focus on the conflicts created by this co-existence, e.g. between Gideon and his father; between traditional and modern attitudes to religion, superstition, relationships etc; between tradition and modern ways of living.

Candidates may choose to answer in bullet points in this final question, or write a number of linked statements. There is no requirement to write a 'mini essay'.

Up to 2 marks can be achieved for identifying elements of **commonality** as identified in the question.

A further 2 marks can be achieved for r**eference to the extract given.**

4 additional marks can be awarded for similar references to **at least one other part of the text** by the writer.

<u>In practice this means:</u>

Identification of commonality (2) (e.g. theme, central relationship, importance of setting, use of imagery, development in characterisation, use of personal experience, use of narrative style, or any other key element ...)

From the extract:

1 relevant reference to technique; 1 appropriate comment

OR 1 relevant reference to idea; 1 appropriate comment

OR 1 relevant reference to feature; 1 appropriate comment

OR 1 relevant reference to text; 1 appropriate comment

(maximum of 2 marks only for discussion of extract)

from at **least one other part of the text:**

as above (×2) for **up to 4 marks**

PART B — PROSE — *The Strange Case of Dr Jekyll and Mr Hyde* **by Robert Louis Stevenson**

23. 1 mark for reference; 1 mark for comment (×2), for a maximum of 4 marks.

    Possible answers include:

    - 'From that time forward' suggests sense of purpose
    - 'haunt (the door)' suggests that he is always there
    - List/'In the morning ...'/'at noon ...'/'at night ...'/'at all hours' suggests that he is searching for Hyde at all times in the day
    - 'before office hours' suggests that he is so keen to find him he starts very early
    - 'under the face of the fogged city moon' suggests that he is not put off by frightening/spooky atmosphere
    - 'by all lights' suggests that he looks for Hyde even when it is dark
    - 'the lawyer was to be found on his chosen spot' suggests that he is always there, looking
    - "'I shall be Mr Seek.'" suggests that he defines his identity by his search for Hyde

24. 1 mark for reference; 1 mark for comment (×2), for a maximum of 4 marks.

    Possible answers include:

    - 'And at last' suggests a long wait
    - 'frost in the air' suggests discomfort
    - 'the streets as clean as a ballroom floor' suggests a space that is (eerily) empty of its usual crowds of people
    - 'shadow' suggests dark presence/hidden danger
    - 'shops were closed' suggests emptiness

- '(very) solitary' suggests isolation
- '(very) silent' suggests a quiet, eerie atmosphere
- Use of 'very'/repetition of 'very' to emphasise the quiet atmosphere
- 'Small sounds carried far'/'low growl of London' suggests menacing setting/threatening noises
- 'rumour' suggests uncertainty
- 'preceded him by a long time' suggests the unseen
- '(Mr. Utterson) had been some minutes at his post' suggests anticipation
- 'an odd, light footstep' suggests the unknown
- 'drawing near' suggests nervousness caused by something approaching
- 'suddenly spring out'/'sharply and decisively arrested' suggests surprise/shock/alert
- 'withdrew (into the entry)' suggests hiding/concealment

25. 1 mark for reference; 1 mark for comment (×2), for a maximum of 4 marks.

Possible answers include:

- '(Mr Hyde) shrank back' suggests that he does not want to be seen/wants to be unknown
- 'hissing (intake of breath)' suggests that there is something inhuman/serpent-like about him/sinister
- 'he did not look the lawyer in the face'/'still without looking up' suggests he is evasive
- 'his fear was only momentary' suggests initial uncertainty/recovers his composure quickly
- 'he answered coolly enough' suggests that there is a confidence about him
- '"How did you know me?"' suggests that he is suspicious
- 'appeared to hesitate' suggests that he is wary
- 'fronted about with an air of defiance' suggests aggression
- 'stared at each other pretty fixedly' suggests he is not afraid

26. Possible areas for comment include:

Extract:

Mr Utterson is clearly trying to seek out a secret in trying so hard to track down Mr Hyde. There are many references within the extract to secrecy, e.g. "I shall be Mr Seek," 'rumour,' 'he withdrew into the entry of the court,' "How did you know me?"

Elsewhere:

The lawyer, Mr Utterson, thinks that Dr Jekyll's will contains a dark secret.

Dr Jekyll conducts secret research in a secret laboratory.

Dr Jekyll keeps the true identity of Mr Hyde hidden.

Dr Jekyll uses the identity of Mr Hyde to keep his own behaviour secret.

Dr Jekyll's servants are sworn to secrecy over the laboratory and the 'existence' of Mr Hyde.

In the novel, secrets are hidden behind doors.

Candidates may choose to answer in bullet points in this final question, or write a number of linked statements. There is no requirement to write a 'mini essay'.

Up to 2 marks can be achieved for identifying elements of **commonality** as identified in the question.

A further 2 marks can be achieved for **reference to the extract given.**

4 additional marks can be awarded for similar references to **at least one other part of the text** by the writer.

In practice this means:

Identification of commonality (2) (e.g. theme, central relationship, importance of setting, use of imagery, development in characterisation, use of personal experience, use of narrative style, or any other key element ...)

From the extract:

1 relevant reference to technique; 1 appropriate comment

OR 1 relevant reference to idea; 1 appropriate comment

OR 1 relevant reference to feature; 1 appropriate comment

OR 1 relevant reference to text; 1 appropriate comment

(maximum of 2 marks only for discussion of extract)

from at **least one other part of the text:**

as above (×2) for **up to 4 marks**

PROSE B — PROSE — *Mother and Son* **by Iain Crichton Smith**

27. 1 mark for reference; 1 mark for comment (×2), for a maximum of 4 marks.

Possible answers include:

- 'subsided'/'"It's only you."' suggests disappointment
- 'relief' suggests she is pleased to see him/glad he is home
- 'contempt' suggests dislike/hatred
- 'acceptance' suggests she puts up with him

28. 1 mark for reference; 1 mark for comment (×2), for a maximum of 4 marks.

Possible answers include:

- '"Well, what's the matter with you!"' suggests aggression/hostility from mother to son
- Exclamation mark suggests anger
- 'snapped' suggests mother's lack of patience
- 'pettishly' suggests mother's sulky/bad-tempered mood
- 'moping' suggests she belittles the importance of his feelings
- 'sigh' suggests dismissiveness/disappointment
- '"... don't know why we christened you John"'/'"My father was never like you."' suggests mother is being provocative
- '"All right, *all* right"' suggests the son is responding to provocation aggressively
- '(he said) despairingly' suggests the son is exhausted with mother's aggression/criticism
- '"Can't you get a new record for your gramophone."'/'"I've heard all this before"'/'"hundreds of times."'/'familiar retort' suggests son is fed up with repetitive nature of mother's critical comments
- 'But she wasn't to be stopped.' suggests mother is keen to continue argument

- "'I can't understand what has come over you lately'" suggests mother is critical of son's present attitude/demeanour
- "'You keep mooning around the house'" suggests the mother is criticising the son for being lazy/trying to start an argument with him
- "'Do you know what's going to happen to you'"/"'you'll be taken to the asylum.'"/derogatory comments about father/father's family suggests insults are intended to provoke
- 'her husband's son, not as her own' suggests she disassociates herself from him

29. 1 mark for reference; 1 mark for comment (×2), for a maximum of 4 marks.

   Possible answers include:

   - 'He pottered about'/'waiting desperately'/'for the sibilant noise to stop' suggests the son is allowing time to pass so that the conflict will be over
   - 'He moved about inside this sea of sound' suggests he feels trapped by the conflict
   - 'trying to keep detached' suggests he tries to shut out the conflict
   - 'trying to force himself from listening' suggests he tries hard not to let it affect him
   - 'burst venomously' suggests a sudden hurt
   - 'out of a clear, cold mind,'/'as if she didn't matter'/'had no meaning for him'/'could not touch him' suggests he tries to ignore his mother
   - 'they stung him'/'stood quivering in his flesh'/'wound' suggests he is poisoned by the conflict/he is deeply hurt by it
   - 'angrily' suggests his temper rises
   - 'reflex'/'He swung round' suggests he responds instinctively
   - 'But she always cornered him' suggests he feels trapped
   - 'He had now become so sensitive' suggests the conflict has made him very anxious/it has affected how he thinks about things
   - 'he usually read some devilish meaning into her smallest utterance.' suggests paranoia/that he demonises her
   - 'he became deferential' suggests he is now submissive

30. *Possible areas for comment include:*

   Extract

   John feels isolated/lonely due to constant tauntings of his mother. He shuts himself off/isolates himself for self-protection.

   The mother feels isolated from John/is lonely when he is away. Her strong feelings are demonstrated in the conflict between John and her, or in her contradictory behaviour towards him — she wants him there, but behaves in a manner which drives him away (adding to her loneliness/isolation).

   Elsewhere:

   Home

   Main character feels isolated from home country when he returns for a visit: "'I wish to God we were home'" (meant ironically). Feels a lack of connection during the visit. Main character and wife are isolated from each other. Wife cuts herself off from the local people: "an empress surrounded by prairie dogs."

   The Telegram

   Isolation of the "thin woman" in the community: "The thin woman was not popular in the village." "She was an incomer ..."

   Isolation and loneliness of the elder at the end of the story as news of the loss of his son is received.

   The Red Door

   Murdo's isolation symbolised by the "Red Door" — he is marked out as different. He could be said to be 'self-isolated': "I have always sought to hide among other people."

   Candidates may choose to answer in bullet points in this final question, or write a number of linked statements. There is no requirement to write a 'mini essay'.

   Up to 2 marks can be achieved for identifying elements of **commonality** as identified in the question.

   A further 2 marks can be achieved for **reference to the extract given.**

   4 additional marks can be awarded for similar references to **at least one other part of the text** by the writer.

   <u>In practice this means:</u>

   Identification of commonality (2) (e.g. theme, central relationship, importance of setting, use of imagery, development in characterisation, use of personal experience, use of narrative style, or any other key element ...)

   From the extract:

   1 relevant reference to technique; 1 appropriate comment

   OR 1 relevant reference to idea; 1 appropriate comment

   OR 1 relevant reference to feature; 1 appropriate comment

   OR 1 relevant reference to text; 1 appropriate comment

   (maximum of 2 marks only for discussion of extract)

   from at **least one other part of the text:**

   as above (×2) for **up to 4 marks**

PART B — PROSE — *Hieroglyphics* by Anne Donovan

31. 1 mark for reference; 1 mark for comment, to a maximum of 2 marks.

   Possible answers include:

   - 'me'/'ma mammy'/'ma sisters'/'Catherine'/'Elizabeth' suggests the awareness of characters as essential elements of a story/she wants her family to be part of her story/she puts real people in her story
   - 'we took nice stuff to eat'/'big plates a mince an tatties'/'ice cream fae the café'/'bottles a ginger and sweeties' suggests she includes detail
   - 'Ah spent a long time thinkin' suggests she invested time/preparation/planning
   - 'So ah decided' suggests the importance of planning (when writing a good story)
   - 'important' suggest awareness of key elements
   - 'three hings' suggests awareness that three is a significant number in storytelling

- 'whit use are CDs …'/'ye widnae want that much stuff'/'that the boat would sink' suggests awareness of need for realism (in a good story)
- 'fairy godmother'/'two blind mice'/'seventeen wee pigs' suggests knowledge of well-known stories/ characters in stories

32. 1 mark for reference; 1 mark for comment, to a maximum of 2 marks.

Possible answers include:

- 'she aye carries'/'a bitty auld blanket roond wi her' suggests awareness of/interest in (Elizabeth's) habits/routine
- 'she'll no go anywhere wioot her teddy'/'Sindy doll' suggests knowledge of what is important (to Elizabeth)
- '(she would need tae take her)' 'teddy'/'new blue jumper' suggests awareness of (Catherine's) favourite possessions
- Reference to 'deelie-boablers' suggests knowledge of (Catherine's) current obsession
- Reference to picture of 'spaniel pup'/'we couldnae huv a real dug doon ma bit' suggests realisation that owning a pet is unrealistic

33. 1 mark for reference; 1 mark for comment (×2), for a maximum of 4 marks.

Possible answers include:

- 'private'/'ah didnae know whit mammy wid take'/'mammys don't tell ye these hings' suggests she is secretive/unrevealing/doesn't share
- 'too busy workin' suggests she is always occupied/ preoccupied with practical things
- 'bringin ye up' suggests she is committed to children
- 'tae huv a loaty time for theirsels' suggests she is unselfish
- 'we are her three best hings'/'Catherine and Elizabeth and me'/reference to list suggests devotion to her children

34. 1 mark for reference; 1 mark for comment (×2), for a maximum of 4 marks.

Possible answers include:

- 'neat wee black drawins' suggests she recognises that her work looks presentable
- 'noticed ah hudny put ma name on it' suggests she wants recognition/doesn't want her work to be anonymous
- '(picture of masel) wi a cheery face on it' suggests positive feelings towards it/sense of satisfaction
- '(pit ma story) right on tap ae the pile' suggests she considers her story to be worth looking at first
- 'centre of his desk' suggests she is so proud of story she wants to draw attention to it

35. *Possible areas for comment include:*

Extract:

Mary is determined to demonstrate that she can learn successfully (Egyptian knowledge), and to show that she can express herself creatively. She is determined to write a good story.

Elsewhere:

All that Glisters

Clare is determined to honour/respect the memory of her father in the way of her choosing/a way that reflects their close bond.

Away in a Manger

Amy is determined to pursue her understanding of the meaning of Christmas through trying to persuade her mother to give shelter to the homeless man.

Dear Santa

Alison is determined to forge a closer relationship with her mother.

Candidates may choose to answer in bullet points in this final question, or write a number of linked statements. There is no requirement to write a 'mini essay'.

Up to 2 marks can be achieved for identifying elements of **commonality** as identified in the question.

A further 2 marks can be achieved for **reference to the extract given**.

4 additional marks can be awarded for similar references to **at least one other part of the text** by the writer.

In practice this means:

Identification of commonality (2) (e.g. theme, central relationship, importance of setting, use of imagery, development in characterisation, use of personal experience, use of narrative style, or any other key element …)

From the extract:

1 relevant reference to technique; 1 appropriate comment

OR 1 relevant reference to idea; 1 appropriate comment

OR 1 relevant reference to feature; 1 appropriate comment

OR 1 relevant reference to text; 1 appropriate comment

(maximum of 2 marks only for discussion of extract)

from at **least one other part of the text:**

as above (×2) for **up to 4 marks**

PART C – POETRY – *The Way My Mother Speaks* by Carol Ann Duffy

36. 1 mark for reference; 1 mark for comment.

Possible answers include:

- 'I say her phrases to myself' suggests she is missing her mother/needs comforted/seeks familiarity
- 'In my head' suggests she feels alone
- 'under the shallows of my breath,' suggests she is anxious
- 'Restful shapes moving' suggests feelings of confusion/disorientation/distance from what is familiar
- 'The day and ever. The day and ever.'/reference to repetition emphasises her feeling of loss as she moves away from her home
- 'The day and ever. The day and ever.'/reference to the rhythm of the train suggests momentum of change/lack of control/inevitability of change
- 'ever' emphasises a feeling of finality of this change

37. 1 mark for refence; 1 mark for comment (×2), up to a maximum of 4 marks.

Possible answers include:

- 'slow evening' suggests time is dragging/ominous/claustrophobic
- 'goes down England' suggests the speaker is lost in a foreign land/descending into the unfamiliar
- 'browsing' suggests searching
- 'the right sky' suggests desire for best fit
- 'too blue' suggests nostalgia for ideal memory
- 'swapped' suggests speed of change/unwelcome change
- 'cool grey' suggests impersonal/miserable/cold/lack of vibrancy
- contrast of 'blue' and 'grey' skies suggests movement towards something less positive
- 'For miles' suggests long journey
- 'What like is it'/'when I think' suggests speaker seeks comfort from Scottish language
- Repetition of 'What like is it' suggests clinging to the past/anxiety/uncertainty
- Repetition/'Nothing is silent. Nothing is not silent' suggests confusion of speaker about leaving home

38. 1 mark for reference; 1 mark for comment (×2), up to a maximum of 4 marks.

Possible answers include:

- 'I am happy and sad' suggests mixed feelings
- 'like a child' suggests innocence
- 'stood' suggests being on the brink of a change in life
- 'end of summer'/reference to seasonal change/beginning of one stage of life and end of another/leaving the more positive stage of life behind/mixed feelings about moving on
- 'dipped a net'/tentative action to explore the new
- 'green' suggests naivety/lack of experience
- 'green, erotic pond' suggests fertility/new life
- 'erotic pond'/exciting and unexplored things to discover

39. 1 mark for each point made.

Possible answers include:

- 'homesick'

  Lonely/she misses the warmth of home and those she loves

  NB: She misses home is acceptable

- 'free'

  Independent/the persona has control over her own life/comfortable with her identity/manages to embrace her past while moving on with her life

- 'in love with the way my mother speaks.'

  Nostalgic/reflects on how much she likes her mother's language

- Generalised/summary answer, e.g. confused/reflective/conflicted

40. Possible areas for comment include:

Extract:

- 'Browsing for the right sky' suggests looking for somewhere to feel at home/feel settled.

  'Too blue swapped for a cool grey' suggests having to adapt to a new environment.

- 'I am happy and sad' suggests conflicting/altered feelings.

- *War Photographer*

  Having to process experiences after changing his surroundings and returning to England.

- *Originally*

  Change as speaker moves and grows up.

- *Mrs Midas*

  Dealing with the change in her husband.

- *In Mrs Tilscher's Class*

  The idea of the excitement and confusion growing up brings.

- *Valentine*

  The speaker changing the conventional view of love.

Candidates may choose to answer in bullet points in this final question, or write a number of linked statements. There is no requirement to write a 'mini essay'.

Up to **2 marks** can be achieved for identifying elements of commonality as requested in the question.

A further **2 marks** can be achieved **for reference to the extract given.**

4 additional marks can be awarded for similar references to **at least one other part of the text.**

<u>In practice this means:</u>

Identification of commonality (2) (e.g. theme, central relationship, importance of setting, use of imagery, development in characterisation, use of personal experience, use of narrative style or any other key element …)

From the extract:

1 × relevant reference to technique

1 × appropriate comment

OR 1 × relevant reference to idea

1 × appropriate comment

OR 1 × relevant reference to feature

1 × appropriate comment

OR 1 × relevant reference to text

1 × appropriate comment

(maximum of **2 marks** only for discussion of extract) **from at least one other part of the text:**

as above (×2) for **up to 4 marks**

PART C — POETRY — *'Glasgow Sonnet i'* by Edwin Morgan

41. mark for reference; 1 mark for comment (×2), up to a maximum of 4 marks.

Possible answers include:

- personification/'mean wind' suggests cruelty
- personification of/'wanders' suggests aimlessness

- 'backcourt trash'/'old mattresses' suggests surroundings are full of rubbish/junk
- 'bric-a-brac' lack of suitable playthings
- 'ash' suggests dirt/connotations of death
- personification/'hackles on puddles' suggests imminent violence/danger
- personification/onomatopoeia/'puff briefly and subside' suggests last gasps of breath before death
- 'play fortresses' suggests even children's games are aggressive/that the people who live in the tenements are under threat
- alliteration/harsh sounds of 'bricks' and 'bric-a-brac' reflects the violence
- rhyme/'trash' and 'ash' emphasises the desolation

  NB: identification of technique without reference. Do not reward the same technique without reference twice.

42. 1 mark for reference; 1 mark for comment (×2), up to a maximum of 4 marks.

Possible answers include:

- 'no windows left to smash' suggests everything has been destroyed
- 'a chipped sill' suggests ruin/inadequate protection
- 'buttresses' suggests need for protection (which is not forthcoming)
- 'last (mistresses)' suggests sense of isolation/clinging on/remaining people standing
- alliteration/'black block' suggests severe, bleak picture
- 'block'/'condemned' suggests idea of an execution
- irony/(ironic use of) 'condemned'/(literal use of) 'condemned to stand' emphasises the unfit state of the building/suggests that being demolished would be better than still existing in this place

43. 1 mark for reference; 1 mark for comment (×2), up to a maximum of 4 marks.

Possible answers include:

- 'the cracks deepen' suggests deterioration of building/breakdown of society
- 'the rats crawl' suggests decay/disease/infestation
- personification/'(the kettle) whimpers' suggests misery/pain/desperation/failing to function
- personification/'crazy (hob)' suggests damaged equipment/lack of stability/lack of control
- juxtaposition/'roses of mould' emphasises the fact that decay is replacing beauty
- 'mould grow' suggests decay is spreading
- 'The man ... has lost his job' suggests he has become useless/hopeless
- 'lies late' suggests the man has no purpose in life/foreshadows death
- 'coughs fall thinly' suggests even his coughs are weak
- personification/'air too poor to rob' suggests the place has nothing to offer/is desperate/pathetic
- enjambment/'coughs fall/thinly into an air too poor to rob' suggests situation is ongoing/never-ending

44. Possible areas for comment include:

    Extract:

    The high level of poverty has affected every aspect of the community, e.g. physical decay, unemployment, lack of hygiene, social breakdown, violence etc.

    In the Snack-bar

    Explores the physical suffering of the old man as he struggles to get to the toilet.

    Explores the suffering of the disabled (in a society where most people are unprepared to help them).

    Glasgow 5 March 1971

    Explores the physical pain the couple go through as they are assaulted.

    Explores the suffering of the innocent at the hands of criminals (in a society where most people are unprepared to help them).

    Trio

    Explores how love and compassion can beat suffering.

    Good Friday

    Explores the potential suffering from the injustice of the class system/a lack of education.

    Winter

    Explores the inevitability of suffering/death.

    Candidates may choose to answer in bullet points in this final question, or write a number of linked statements. There is no requirement to write a 'mini essay'.

    Up to **2 marks** can be achieved for identifying elements of commonality as requested in the question.

    A further **2 marks** can be achieved for **reference to the extract given.**

    4 additional marks can be awarded for similar references to **at least one other poem by Morgan.**

    In practice this means:

    Identification of commonality (2) (e.g.: theme, central relationship, importance of setting, use of imagery, development in characterisation, use of personal experience, use of narrative style or any other key element ...)

    From the extract:

    1 × relevant reference to technique

    1 × appropriate comment

    OR 1 × relevant reference to idea

    1 × appropriate comment

    OR 1 × relevant reference to feature

    1 × appropriate comment

    OR 1 × relevant reference to text

    1 × appropriate comment

    (maximum of 2 marks only for discussion of extract) from at least one other poem:

    as above (×2) for up to **4 marks**

PART C — POETRY — *Brooklyn cop* by Norman MacCaig

45. 1 mark for reference; 1 mark for comment (×2), up to a maximum of 4 marks.

Possible answers include:

- 'Built like a gorilla' suggests fierce/violent nature/physically strong/imposing size/dehumanised

- 'but less timid' suggests he is even more frightening/outgoing than this animal/will not be held back/brave/aggressive

- 'thick-fleshed' suggests physical strength/difficult to hurt or to cause him pain/resilient

- 'steak coloured' suggests that he is on the streets in all weathers/weather beaten/unhealthy lifestyle/effects of the job

- '(two) hieroglyphs (in his face)' suggests facial scars/not easy to read

- '(two) hieroglyphs (in his face) that mean trouble' suggests a long history of policing in the area/that he is always looking for danger

46. 1 mark for reference; 1 mark for comment (×2), up to a maximum of 4 marks.

Possible answers include:

- 'See you babe'/'wife'/'honey' suggests loving relationship

- repetition/'he hoped it, he truly hoped it' suggests the constant threat that he might not return alive

- '"Hiya, honey' is no cliché" suggests that he is glad to return home/glad to return to safety

47. 1 mark for reference; 1 mark for comment (×2), up to a maximum of 4 marks.

Possible answers include:

- Question suggests the violence/lack of safety in the job

- 'who would be him' suggests the idea that no one envies his job due to the danger

- paradox/'gorilla with a nightstick' suggests that in this society even this strong and threatening man needs further protection/truncheon/weapon

- 'nightstick' suggests inadequate protection against greater dangers

- 'whose home (is a place he might, this time,) never get back to?' suggests the threat that he might die while doing his job/he might not return to his house and family

- parenthesis/'this time' suggests he is not as confident as he seems/highlights his worries

48. 1 mark for reference; 1 mark for comment.

Possible answers include:

- 'And who would be' refers back to 'Who would be him'

- 'And who would be' refers back to idea of empathy with characters

- 'who' refers back to idea of faceless/unknown aggressors

- 'have to be' refers back to violent society/ever present threat of violence (for the cop or public)

- 'who would be who would have to be' refers back to structure of 'he hoped it, he truly hoped it'

- 'his victims' introduces a role reversal of the earlier idea of the cop as threatened individual/provides a twist/empathy with characters

- use of question/example of question repeats earlier use of question/questioning tone

- enjambement/example of enjambement refers back to earlier use of enjambement

49. Possible areas for comment include:

Extract:

Reference to violent society.

'Should the tissue tear,' 'whose home (is a place he might, this time,) never get back to, 'what clubbings,' 'gunshots,' 'gorilla with a nightstick' 'his victims'.

All suggest the prevalence of violence in society.

Assisi

The less fortunate being ignored by the tourists and the church/the importance of inner beauty.

Visiting Hour

Loss of a loved one or relationship/slow decaying process of death/hopelessness felt by relatives/despair at loss of communication.

Basking Shark

Realisation of man's inhumanity/false sense of superiority/separation from nature.

Aunt Julia

Loss of a loved one/inability to communicate with others/regret at lack of actions.

Hotel Room 12th Floor

The night-time noises and violence of the city/fear.

Candidates may choose to answer in bullet points in this final question, or write a number of linked statements. There is no requirement to write a 'mini essay'.

Up to **2 marks** can be achieved for identifying elements of commonality as requested in the question.

A further **2 marks** can be achieved for **reference to the extract given**.

4 additional marks can be awarded for similar references to **at least one other poem by MacCaig.**

In practice this means:

Identification of commonality (2) (e.g.: theme, central relationship, importance of setting, use of imagery, development in characterisation, use of personal experience, use of narrative style or any other key element ...)

From the extract:

1 × relevant reference to technique

1 × appropriate comment

OR 1 × relevant reference to idea

1 × appropriate comment

OR 1 × relevant reference to feature

1 × appropriate comment

OR 1 × relevant reference to text

1 × appropriate comment

(maximum of 2 marks only for discussion of extract)

from at **least one other poem**:

as above (×2) for **up to 4 marks**

50. 1 mark for reference; 1 mark for comment (×2), up to a maximum of 4 marks.

Possible answers include:

- 'dragging me along' suggests reluctance
- (to the) 'strange place' suggests unfamiliarity
- 'where the air is trapped' suggests discomfort
- 'and ghosts sit at the altar' suggests uneasiness in spirituality
- emphatic statement/'My parents do not believe.' suggests parents do not agree with going to church
- monosyllabic sentence/'It is down to her.' suggests dutiful behaviour of Grandmother (in attending church)
- 'A couple of prayers/A hymn or two.' suggests lack of genuine interest/commitment to religion/only does it to please her gran
- 'Threepenny bit in the collection hat.' suggests token donation of money
- simile/'A flock of women ... flapping over me like missionaries' suggests feeling stifled
- 'and that is that' suggests relief when the service is over
- 'until the next time' reference to inevitability of time interrupting life suggests intrusive nature of religion
- 'God grabs me' suggests forced attendance/no choice

51. 1 mark for reference; 1 mark for comment (×2), up to a maximum of 4 marks.

Possible answers include:

- 'we are almost the same height' suggests physical similarities/longevity of relationship
- 'She still walks faster (rushing me down ...)' suggests the speaker was holding the Grandmother back
- 'I start to pick some notes (oh can you wash a sailor's shirt ...) and/or (Someone's crying my Lord Kumbaya)' suggests the Grandmother has taught the speaker some music
- 'till my gran comes running/I told you don't touch anything.' suggests the Grandmother is a disciplinarian
- simile/'like the hunchback of Notre Dame' suggests the speaker realises that her Grandmother is not as strong as she once was
- '... she slaps me./Sit up straight' suggests the Grandmother encourages good posture/behaviour

52. (a) 1 mark for reference; 1 mark for comment.

Possible answers include:

Word choice:

- 'High Street' suggests it is prestigious
- 'The hall is huge.' suggests scale/enormity
- simile/'Rooms lead off like an octopus's arms' suggests the exoticness/unfamiliarity of layout/complexity

- personification/'grand piano ... one-winged creature' continues the idea of grandness/the exotic/wealth
- 'polishes for hours' suggests the size of house/the level of cleaning required
- 'don't touch anything' suggests there are expensive items

Sentence structure:

- monosyllabic sentence/'The hall is huge.' suggests being overwhelmed/speechless by the scale
- use of dash/'top open — a one-winged creature' suggests wonderment

(b) 1 mark for reference; 1 mark for comment.

Possible answers include:

Word choice:

- 'the posh one all smiles' suggests a false kindness/royal or regal
- 'goosepimples (run up my arms)' suggests nervousness/intimidation
- 'Lovely she says' suggests lack of genuineness
- 'skin the colour of café au lait' condescending/judgmental/pompous attitude

Sentence structure:

- use of question/'Would you like to sing me a song?' suggests she is patronising
- repetition/monosyllabic sentence/'Not at all. Not at all.' suggests she does not want to become involved in conversation/aloofness/dismissiveness
- monosyllabic/abrupt sentence/'You just get back to your work.' suggests impatience/bossy attitude

53. **Extract:**

- Strong feelings of admiration towards her grandmother.
- Strong feelings of overpowering religious routine.
- Strong feelings of social difference.
- *Old Tongue*

  Feelings of powerlessness because she is forced/compelled to move from Scotland to England against her will. Feelings of distress as she feels like she is losing touch with her Scottish identity.
- *Whilst Leila Sleeps*

  Feelings of fear/terror/distress as the speaker is fleeing her home/is seized by the authorities.
- *Gap Year*

  Feelings of happiness in the mother about what the son has achieved/experienced despite the fact that she misses him as he is far away.
- *Keeping Orchids*

  Feelings of frustration/dissatisfaction/anger in the speaker who wants to understand the truth of her early life when she was given away.
- *Lucozade*

  Mixed feelings caused by hospitalisation, illness and then possible recovery.

A further **2 marks** can be achieved for reference **to the extract given**.

4 additional marks can be awarded for similar references to at least **one other text/part of the text** by the writer.

<u>In practice this means:</u>

Identification of commonality (2) (e.g. theme, central relationship, importance of setting, use of imagery, development in characterisation, use of personal experience, use of narrative style, or any other key element …)

From the extract:

1 × relevant reference to technique

1 × appropriate comment

OR 1 × relevant reference to idea

1 × appropriate comment

OR

1 × relevant reference to feature

1 × appropriate comment

OR

1 × relevant reference to text

1 × appropriate comment

(maximum of 2 marks only for discussion of extract)

from at **least one other text:**

as above (×2) for **up to 4 marks**

SECTION 2 – CRITICAL ESSAY

Please see the assessment criteria for the Critical Essay on page 127.

Plot, character and setting

4

Through the author's eyes

> **Objectives:** To identify how characters are built up from small details, and how the reader responds to them.
> **What you need:** Copies of *The Twits*, photocopiable page 15, writing materials.
> **Cross-curricular links:** Art and design.

What to do
● Read the first chapter with the children. Ask if there is anything to suggest this is fiction. Does it use past tense story-telling language? Discuss how the use of the present tense gives a contrasting non-fiction feel to the text. What suppositions does the author make about beard wearers? (Be sensitive to children whose fathers may have beards out of choice or for religious reasons.)
● Explain that this 'stand-alone' diatribe acts as a foreword. Ask the children to read the next two chapters. Discuss the purpose of Chapter 1 in the context of what follows (to prejudice the reader against beards). Point out that the author next describes one specific beard and its owner's habits.
● Ask the children to complete photocopiable page 15, to compare the author's general opinions with his specific detailed description of Mr Twit.
● Encourage the children to consider other novels they have read. Do all authors present such a strongly biased viewpoint in the telling of their stories? What is the effect of such an opinionated narrator?

> **Differentiation**
> **For older/more able children:** Ask the children to write a general, positive paragraph about beards (present tense) and a descriptive paragraph (past tense).
> **For younger/less able children:** Let the children draw a likeable character and label the beard in positive terms.

The first four tricks

> **Objective:** To consider credibility of events, comparing fiction to real life.
> **What you need:** Copies of *The Twits*, individual whiteboards, copies of Extract 1, page 8 (differentiation only), different coloured pens.
> **Cross-curricular links:** History.

What to do
● Ask the children to read from 'The Glass Eye' to 'The Funny Walking-stick'.
● Invite the children to share examples of practical jokes they have experienced or played.
● Ask the children to compile two lists of possible results of such tricks – *Intentional results* (to make people jump, make others laugh) and *Unintentional results* (break a bone, have a heart attack). Establish that tricks played with harmful intent are malicious.
● Discuss the Twits' tricks. Which sound plausible? Invite the children to consider the level of harm each trick causes. Which is the worst trick? Why?
● Encourage the children to connect the tricks, showing how one trick leads to another, setting the tone and developing the plot. Ask them to draw a time line with arrows indicating the 'knock-on' effect of one trick to the next.
● Encourage the children to write down what they think might happen next. Which Twit do they think will succeed in outwitting the other?

> **Differentiation**
> **For older/more able children:** Ask the children to write about another trick that either of the Twits might play on the other.
> **For younger/less able children:** Distribute copies of Extract 1. Ask the children to underline phrases that show Mrs Twit's practical deceit, and, in a different colour, phrases that show Mr Twit's plotting.

Plot, character and setting

Reading between the lines

> **Objective:** To investigate how characters are presented through dialogue.
> **What you need:** Copies of *The Twits*, paper and pens.

What to do

● Ask the children to read up to the end of 'Mrs Twit Goes Ballooning Up'. Explain that what someone *says* and what they *mean* can be quite different – sometimes exactly the *opposite*. Elicit that this is called sarcasm.
● Ask the children to re-read the chapter 'Mrs Twit Goes Ballooning Up'. Explain that the children are going to 'translate' each direct speech to show what the speaker is really saying, or else explain how they know that the words are meant to be taken literally.

● Ask each child to make a table with three columns under the following headings: 'What the person is saying', 'What they mean', and 'Sarcasm or exaggeration?'.
● Tell the children to write each speech they can find in this chapter under the first heading. They should then fill in the other two columns for each speech. For example: 'There's…moon', means that there is a strong pull, it's an exaggeration.
● Share the findings and discuss how the children could tell if it was sarcasm or a literal meaning.

> **Differentiation**
> Use the written findings as a basis of a presentation, pairing more able and less able children together: the former as translators, the latter reading the quotations from the text.

Just typical!

> **Objective:** To investigate how characters are presented, referring to the text.
> **What you need:** Copies of *The Twits*, photocopiable page 16, writing materials, flipchart.

What to do

● Remind the children of the chapter 'The Frog'. Write on the flipchart: 'Dirty old hags like her always have itchy tummies.'
● Establish that it is a general statement that implies application to one specific person. Who does the 'like her' refer to? (Mrs Twit.)
● Discuss why the author includes this statement. (To influence the reader's opinion of Mrs Twit.) How does it help establish the nature of the character? (By implication.) Ask the children what is implied by the statement. (Unwashed skin will itch therefore Mrs Twit is *dirty*; dirt on skin smells so Mrs Twit is *smelly*.)
● Draw attention to these final adjectives (dirty, smelly), revealed through implication and deduction. Write them in a statement,

underlining the adjectives: Mrs Twit is <u>dirty</u> and <u>smelly</u>. Stress how the reader knows these adjectives describe Mrs Twit, even when the text does not use these words.
● Discuss *why* the author uses implication, rather than a direct statement. (For example, it is more subtle.)
● Ask the children to use photocopiable page 16 to reveal what is implied by further such statements about Mr and Mrs Twit.
● Once the children have completed their photocopiable sheets, ask some of them to share their adjectives. Compile these on the board to provide a comprehensive list about these two characters. What does it tell you?

> **Differentiation**
> **For older/more able children:** Ask the children to find some characteristic-revealing quotations for other characters.
> **For younger/less able children:** Create some adjective word cards for the children to match up to the quotations on the photocopiable sheet.

Plot, character and setting

Word pictures

Objective: To investigate how and to what effect figurative language is used and locate similes.
What you need: Copies of *The Twits*, individual whiteboards, pens.

What to do

● Use this activity when the children have finished the book.
● Quentin Blake's illustrations are integral to the text. Point out examples, such as Mrs Twit's face growing ugly over time (in 'Mrs Twit').
● Point out that words can also be used to paint pictures, by the use of similes. Write the following list on the board and ask the children to locate and note down, on their whiteboards, the respective similes:
  ● Mr Twit's beard
  ● good thoughts in a person's face
  ● Mr Twit's pointing finger
  ● a feature of the Skillywaggler
  ● Mrs Twit's skirt as she comes ballooning down
  ● Mr Twit's reaction to Mrs Twit's return.
● Discuss how these similes affect the descriptions. (They make them more vivid.)
● Encourage the children to find the simile in 'The Glass Eye'. ('I watch you like a wombat.') What is unusual about it? (Wombats can't see very well.)
● Invite the children to invent further similes inspired by studying the illustrations.

Differentiation
For older/more able children: Challenge the children to locate and explain the metaphor in 'Four Sticky Little Boys' ('…their naked bottoms winking at the sun.').
For younger/less able children: Write the list on separate cards, including chapter references.

Atmosphere and tension

Objective: To explore the build-up of tension and atmosphere with close reference to the text.
What you need: Copies of *The Twits*, writing materials.
Cross-curricular links: Art and design.

What to do

● Invite the children to read 'The Great Glue Painting Begins'. Discuss how events develop Muggle-Wump's character.
● Ask the children to consider the effect of alliteration and irony. Encourage the children to compare this lengthier speech with the following dialogue. How do they interpret the breathless brevity of Muggle-Wump's speeches and use of exclamation marks? (Sense of urgency; excitement.)
● Point out the imperative verbs: 'Come on', 'Jump', 'Stand', 'Hop'. Invite a confident reader to read aloud Muggle-Wump's speech following '…frenzy of excitement', to demonstrate how short lines speed up narrative, increasing a sense of urgency.
● Ask what inferences can be made from the reaction of Muggle-Wump's children? (They are slower and less excited than their father.)
● Why does the author use dialogue rather than description? (Hastens the action; reinforces the atmosphere of panic.) Ask the children to explore the meaning of 'frenzy' and to write a paragraph on Muggle-Wump's emotional state of mind, referring to the text.

Differentiation
For older/more able children: Ask the children to explain what effect Muggle-Wump's lack of explanation to the younger monkeys has on the reader. (Increases curiosity to read on.)
For younger/less able children: Let the children draw the four monkeys, adding speech bubbles and direct-speech quotations.

Plot, character and setting

Different voices

> **Objective:** To look at how dialogue is presented in stories, identifying different voices.
> **What you need:** Copy of *The Twits* for each pair of children, enlarged copy of Extract 2 (page 9), photocopiable page 17.

What to do
● Ask the children to read 'Mrs Twit Has the Shrinks' in pairs.
● Display the enlarged extract. Point out the layout and punctuation of the direct speech. Discuss how it helps to show that Mr Twit is speaking each time in his description of the shrinks, and helps to describe the manner in which he delivers his speech.
● Let each pair of children re-read the direct speeches in role, as Mr or Mrs Twit respectively. Choose a pair to perform to the rest of the class.
● Invite the children to read the final chapter of the book 'The Twits Get the Shrinks'. Compare the chapter titles, the nature of the shrinks and the direct speech. (Now 'real shrinks' where previously a trick; earlier, Mr Twit is in control, whereas at the end it is 'each man for himself'!)
● Discuss whether the punishment fits the crime.
● Hand out photocopiable page 17 and ask the children to explain the events leading to the Twits' downfall, with reference to previous events and dialogue.
● Discuss their responses as a class.

> **Differentiation**
> **For older/more able children:** Challenge the children to create a similar chart for the monkeys that shows how their fortunes improve.
> **For younger/less able children:** Blank out the 'Like when…' sections of the photocopiable sheet to simplify it.

Fewer chapters

> **Objective:** To understand how chapters are used to collect, order and build up ideas.
> **What you need:** Copies of *The Twits*, writing materials, photocopiable page 18.

What to do
● Use this activity once the children have finished the book.
● Ask the children to look at the contents list. Elicit that these divisions are called chapters, and that they help the reader to navigate the book. How do the chapters in *The Twits* differ from chapters in other books? (No numbering; very short; very specific.)
● Discuss how much of the plot is revealed in the titles alone. (For example, we can see that, after 'Mrs Twit Goes Ballooning Up', she will come down again.)
● Ask the children to discuss in pairs where the story changes direction, such as, from introducing characters by appearance to progressing to their behaviour; from trick-playing reaching new levels of cruelty to introducing the monkeys.
● Give out the photocopiable sheet and ask the children to divide the narrative into fewer, longer chapters, inventing an appropriate, broader title for each, and summing up the plot development of each new chapter.
● As a class, discuss the children's chapter ideas. Why did they decide to split them like this? What titles did they use? Talk about the effects and benefits, or disadvantages, of longer or shorter chapters.

> **Differentiation**
> **For older/more able children:** Ask the children to quote a pivotal line from each 'new chapter' which shows the story is moving on to a fresh phase.
> **For younger/less able children:** Provide a full contents list for them to cut up and sequence.

Plot, character and setting

SECTION
4

Through the author's eyes

Imagine you are interviewing Roald Dahl and Mr Twit. Show how their answers to similar questions will differ. Finally, re-read the first three chapters and write your own question and their replies.

Mr Dahl, I think you do not trust a man with a beard. Why not?

Why don't you like Mr Twit's beard?

Roald Dahl

Mr Twit

What do you think your beard does for you, Mr Twit?

How often do you wash your beard?

Illustration © Quentin Blake

My own question: _____

_____ ?

Roald Dahl

Mr Twit

Plot, character and setting

Just typical!

For each quotation, write what it implies and the adjectives that can be used to describe the character. The first one has been done for you.

Character	Quotation	What is implied	Adjectives
Illustration © Quentin Blake	People like her always have itchy tummies. …opened her big mouth and said something silly. She was very good at growing thistles and stinging-nettles.	Her tummy itches as she does not wash. Dirt smells.	Mrs Twit is…<u>dirty</u>, <u>smelly</u>.
Illustration © Quentin Blake	He wiped the white froth on to his sleeve. …kept them practising for six hours every day. He loved Bird Pie. It was his favourite meal.		Mr Twit is…

Plot, character and setting

Different voices

For each stage of their downfall, write:

1) how and what happened to the Twits

2) whether what happened was similar to any other incident

3) what one of the Twits said to show how they felt.

Illustration © Quentin Blake

The Twits are…

…firstly, fooled	…secondly, manipulated
How?	How?
Like when…	Like when…
Mr/Mrs Twit said:	Mr/Mrs Twit said:

…then, trapped	…and, finally, destroyed.
How?	How?
Like when…	Like when…
Mr/Mrs Twit said:	Mr/Mrs Twit said:

SECTION
4

Fewer chapters

Divide *The Twits* into fewer, longer chapters. Invent a new title for each and sum up the plot development.

NOTE: *YOU* decide how many chapters you need.

REMEMBER: They do not all have to be the same length. Most will be longer but some may stay as they are if you wish.

New chapter number	Covering pages from… to…	New chapter title	Short notes of story content
For example **1**	p1–p8	The Hairy Scary Twits	Talking about beards and introducing the two main characters.
2	p9–p…		

Continue on the other side if you run out of space.

Talk about it

Like it or loathe it?

Objective: To evaluate a book by referring to details and examples in the text.
What you need: Copies of *The Twits*, writing materials, photocopiable page 22.
Cross-curricular links: Citizenship; Art and design.

What to do
● Arrange the class in pairs. Hand out the photocopiable sheet and copies of *The Twits*.
● Tell the pairs to read and discuss the comments in the light of the three questions at the top of the photocopiable sheet.
● Bring the class together to share their responses to the comments and to evaluate their usefulness. Ask questions such as: 'Which comments made reference to the book's plot?' and, 'Who used quotations from the text?'.
● Now ask the pairs to use the comments as a starting point to discuss *The Twits*, as if they were taking part in a radio or television debate. Explain that their comments should be helpful to someone trying to decide whether or not to read the book. One child should take the role of a critic who enjoyed the book, the other a critic who did not. Encourage the children to challenge each other's opinions.
● Choose pairs to present their debates to the class.

Differentiation
For older/more able children: Encourage the children to create a visual aid for their presentation, such as a notice with the author's name, ISBN and price.
For younger/less able children: Allow the children to underline comments from the photocopiable sheet that they agree with. They can then incorporate these into their debate.

Matching names and natures

Objective: To collaborate with others to plan stories in chapters, aimed at readers who enjoyed *The Twits*.
What you need: Individual whiteboards and writing materials.

What to do
● As a whole class, discuss how Mr and Mrs Twit live up to their name: their horrible tricks, making monkeys do silly things, not learning from experience, thinking dirty beards look wise.
● Ask the children to say which they think came first in Roald Dahl's mind: the characters, the setting or the plot? (The opening tirade against beards could suggest Mr Twit's character came first.) Discuss how his character might, in turn, dictate Mrs Twit's. How are other characters likely to react to them?
● Brainstorm names and matching characteristics, from which the children may develop characters, setting and events to form a plot. For example, Mr and Mrs Brain who invent clever machines to help people.
● Using *The Twits* format as a model (introduction, scene-setting, wider impact, crisis, resolution), ask the children, in groups, to plan a downfall or a triumph for their chosen characters, using their behavioural traits to influence events. They should plan their story in chapters with notes of main events.
● Ask a spokesman from each group to present their proposals. Invite members of different groups to offer constructive comments. What do they think of the characters' names and characteristics? In what respects is the proposal similar to *The Twits*?

Differentiation
For older/more able children: Ask the children to write an opening paragraph to introduce the characters.
For younger/less able children: Have an adult act as prompt and scribe for the children's planning.

Talk about it

Adapted for stage

Objective: To develop playscripts.
What you need: Copies of *The Twits*, photocopiable page 23.
Cross-curricular links: PE; Drama.

What to do
● Explain that *The Twits* was adapted as a series of children's plays by David Wood. They contain much narration and many of the actions that take place in the novel are modified.
● Hand out the photocopiable sheet. Ask the children to read it in pairs and locate and compare it to the content in the original story ('The Funny Walking-stick'). What differences can they find? (The stick gets suddenly shorter instead of gradually longer; Mr Twit convinces Mrs Twit she is growing rather than shrinking.)
● Discuss the necessity for these changes to overcome difficult – or impossible – situations.

● Ask the children to look closely at the script. Do they think the words convey the characters accurately, even if differing in detail? How has David Wood retained the spirit of the original plot and characterisation?
● Divide the class into groups of six. Ask them to improvise the monkeys being made to perform by the Twits, taking a role each (four monkeys and Mr and Mrs Twit). Then ask them to plan a circus-style routine and dialogue to convey the spirit of the chapter entitled 'Mr and Mrs Twit Go Off to Buy Guns'.
● Ask the groups to perform to the rest of the class. What have they changed?

Differentiation
For older/more able children: Ask the children to improvise a script to accompany their performance.
For younger/less able children: Provide extra adult help.

Who's the bully?

Objective: To identify issues in stories.
What you need: Copies of *The Twits*, photocopiable page 24.
Cross-curricular links: PSHE; Drama; Citizenship, Unit 07, Children's rights – human rights.

What to do
● Propose that, although treated humorously, *The Twits* is a story about bullying. Mr and Mrs Twit bully each other and torment anything in their control. Discuss bullying together.
● Ask the children to imagine that Mrs Twit decides to take Mr Twit to court, accusing him of bullying. Mr Twit says in his defence that *she* bullied *him*.
● Organise the children into two groups. Select two in each group to role-play Mr and Mrs Twit, another two to act as courtroom barristers. Ask other children to role-play witnesses (a boy, bird, monkey and so on).

● Hand out the photocopiable sheet to help the groups prepare their case to defend or accuse Mr Twit.
● You (or another adult) should act as the judge. Explain that you will be assessing the case on the strength of argument and evidence provided.
● Create a simple courtroom and choose one group to lead the role-play sessions.
● Ask the role-play 'lawyers' to present their case. After each has had their turn, invite them back to counter-argue or call back witnesses.
● Sum up the children's points, before finding Mr Twit guilty or not guilty in both groups' role-play scenario.

Differentiation
For older/more able children: Invite 12 children to act as a jury.
For younger/less able children: Act as defence or prosecution barrister to pose questions for the children to answer in role.

Talk about it

Dad's gone mad!

> **Objective:** To tell a story orally.
> **What you need:** Copies of *The Twits*.
> **Cross-curricular links:** Drama.

What to do

● Use this activity after the children have read how Muggle-Wump has organised his family and the Roly-Poly Bird into turning the Twits' living-room upside down.
● Ask the children to re-read 'The Great Glue Painting Begins' to the end of 'The Furniture Goes Up', particularly noting the young monkeys' and the Roly-Poly Bird's reactions to Muggle-Wump's orders. Invite children to read aloud the monkeys' comments about their dad's behaviour, putting expression into their voice. Remind the children to stress words in italics.
● Elicit why Muggle-Wump does not stop to explain his plan but simply issues orders. (He is in too much of a hurry.)

● Arrange the children in pairs. Ask one of the children in each pair to tell the story, of what happened from a young monkey's point of view, to their partner. Offer the title: 'Dad's gone mad!' Explain that they will need to speak in the first person, in the persona of a child monkey.
● After a few minutes, ask the children to swap speaking and listening roles, allowing the second 'monkey' to give their perspective of events – possibly embellishing the first child's description.
● Ask the children to perform their role-plays to the rest of the class.

> **Differentiation**
> **For older/more able children:** Encourage the children to retell their stories to the whole class. Be prepared to use prompt questions.
> **For younger/less able children:** Help the children to identify direct speech and turn it into reported actions.

Baked in a pie

> **Objectives:** To identify social, moral or cultural issues in stories, and to discuss how the characters deal with them.
> **What you need:** Flipchart and pen.
> **Cross-curricular links:** Citizenship, Unit 02, Choices; History.

What to do

● Remind the children of the rhyme 'Sing a Song of Sixpence', reflecting how, in former times, people did eat small birds in pies, just as the Twits do. Briefly discuss the way in which people's attitudes change over time.
● Explain that we can use terms such as 'What if…?' to examine issues through asking ourselves questions.
● Sort the children into groups of six to discuss the moral, social and cultural issues in the story. Write discussion springboards on a flipchart, such

as: should we be allowed to eat what we like?
● Compare findings as a class. Highlight how attitudes differ according to era and culture. Is the reader influenced by the anthropomorphism of the animals in this story?
● Ask the children to consider the Bird Pie in relation to other evidence of the Twits' attitudes. What if they *had* caught the boys?
● Finally, discuss the story's ending. Was it fair? What other endings might have given the Twits a taste of their own medicine? (Being put in a pie?) Is it justifiable to treat people in the same bad way that they treated others?

> **Differentiation**
> **For older/more able children:** Ask groups to make a presentation of their findings.
> **For younger/less able children:** Monitor the discussion closely, ensuring the children explore different possibilities.

Talk about it

Like it or loathe it?

Below are some children's opinions of Roald Dahl's book, *The Twits*.
Who do you think makes a good point?
Which points do you disagree with?
Which children explained their opinions well?

Abi: *The Twits* was a silly book. It made me feel sick reading about the food in Mr Twit's beard.

Daisy: I thought the book was very funny. The tricks they played reminded me of tricks that I'd like to play on my brother but wouldn't dare. I didn't care how nasty they were, once I knew that the monkeys and birds would get their revenge.

Ben: I liked the short chapters. It made it easy to read. My favourite chapter was 'Mrs Twit Comes Ballooning Down'. I could just picture thousands of birds 'flying in from miles around to stare at this extraordinary old woman in the sky'.

Ella: I didn't like the book very much except for the rhymes that the Roly-Poly Bird made up to sing. And I liked the funny names they called The Twits, like 'fearful frumptious freaks'.

Carl: Mr and Mrs Twit were great. I mean, they're horrible, really, but they were well drawn by the illustrator. That was because Roald Dahl described them in such detail. I could really imagine the faces they pulled and hear their voices.

Fatima: When I got to the end of the book I shouted 'Hooray', too.

Gaz: Roald Dahl is a wizard with words – especially made-up ones. His characters are larger than life (except when they shrink). It's the best book I've read since my last Roald Dahl book!

Harry: The Twits are not quite believable but they are real enough that you can make yourself believe in them. They hate children, which is why I hated them and was glad when they got their come-uppance. Thanks to the clever Roly-Poly Bird and the brave monkeys, they came to a very bad end. It was a good end, I think!

Make notes on the other side of this sheet to prepare for a debate, explaining reasons why you like or dislike the book. Find evidence and quotations from the book to support your opinions.

Adapted for stage

[MR TWIT *unfreezes and tiptoes to* MRS TWIT, *putting his finger to his lips as if to tell the audience not to say anything. Unseen by* MRS TWIT, *he snaps off half of her walking stick. He hands it to an* ACTOR *or* STAGE MANAGER, *then takes, from another* ACTOR *or* STAGE MANAGER, *two glasses of beer. He sits at the table.*]

MR TWIT: [*Warmly*] A glass of beer, my dear?

[MRS TWIT *unfreezes*]

MRS TWIT: Mmmm. Lovely. [*She goes to walk, using her stick, but it is so short she crashes to the floor*]

[MR TWIT *laughs*]

Aaaah! [*She struggles up, forced to stoop because of the short walking stick*] What's happened?

[MR TWIT *quickly removes his shoes, kneels down into them and shuffles towards her*]

MR TWIT: You seem to be growing, my sweet.

MRS TWIT: Growing?

MR TWIT: [*Arriving and looking shorter than her*] Growing. Take a look at your stick, you old goat, and see how much you've grown in comparison.

MRS TWIT: [*Looking at her stick in amazement*] Never!

MR TWIT: You always said you wanted me to look up to you! Your wish has been granted.

MRS TWIT: I don't want to grow!

MR TWIT: No?

MRS TWIT: No! Do something!

MR TWIT: Do something? Anything?

MRS TWIT: Anything! Stop me growing!

MR TWIT: Of course, my pet.

[MR TWIT *stands up, unseen by* MRS TWIT, *and fetches an enormous joke mallet, which he brings crashing down on her head*]

MRS TWIT: Aaah!

[MR TWIT *laughs and, seen by* MRS TWIT, *takes the bottom half of her walking stick from the* ACTOR *or* STAGE MANAGER *and replaces it*]

MR TWIT: Just a little joke, my honey-bunny!

An extract of 'Meet the Twits' from *The Twits – Plays for children* by Roald Dahl adapted by David Wood
© 2003 David Wood (2003 Puffin)

Who's the bully?

Defendant in court: **Name:** Mr Twit

Age: 60+

Charged with
Bullying Mrs Twit

Prosecutor in court: **Name:** Mrs Twit

Age: 60+

Claims to be
The Innocent
Victim
of Bullying

Illustration © Quentin Blake

Points in support of Mrs Twit's accusation:

Points to use in Mr Twit's defence:

Get writing

Payback time

> **Objectives:** To plan a story; to write a new scene into a story, in the manner of the writer.
> **What you need:** Copies of *The Twits*, whiteboards and pens, flipchart.

What to do

- Use this activity after the children have read to the end of 'Mr Twit Gets a Horrid Shock'.
- Remind the children of the words: 'To pay Mr Twit back…' and 'To pay Mrs Twit back…', setting the tit-for-tat tone to the couple's relationship.
- Read the opening paragraph of 'The House, the Tree and the Monkey Cage'. Draw attention to the repeated adjective 'disgusting'.
- Ask the children to imagine what the next trick might have been had the author not changed the course of the narrative. Whose turn is it to play a revenge trick? (Mrs Twit's.)
- Tell the children that they are going to plan another trick for Mrs Twit to play on Mr Twit.
- Invite the children to suggest strategies, referring to past tricks, such as: plotting, preparation, subterfuge, timing, intention. Remind them that the trick must match the others in terms of plausibility, and be *disgusting*.
- Identify characters' typical phrases and characteristics. Record suggestions on the board.
- Now ask the children to write notes for the chapter in which their trick will take place.

> **Differentiation**
> **For older/more able children:** Ask the children to write their episode as a short additional chapter based on their notes.
> **For younger/less able children:** Help the children to create a storyboard and brief notes.

The dreaded shrinks

> **Objective:** To write clear instructions.
> **What you need:** Copies of *The Twits*, examples of instructional texts, flipchart, paper, writing materials, computers (optional).
> **Cross-curricular links:** ICT; Art and design.

What to do

- Ask the children to consider what Mr and Mrs Twit are good at. (Planning tricks.) Explain that some people share personal expertise and talents through writing articles, for example: 'How to bake bread'.
- Share examples, drawing attention to organisational devices, such as: numbered lists, bullet points and sub-headings. Ask the children to consider: text length; lists of required materials; inclusion of safety tips.
- Tell the children that they are going to be Mr Twit, writing instructions on how to make a person think that they are shrinking. Discuss what this will include in the context of the instructional texts discussed – drawing on the story text.
- With the children's help, list stages on a flipchart, including: victim selection, preparations and what to do.
- Remind the children that they will need a title, such as: 'How to fool a friend into believing they have the dreaded shrinks'. Suggest they could also use sub-headings.
- Are there safety points that should be included? Invite suggestions as to how to display them. (In a text box, bold font.)
- Now ask the children to write their own set of instructions, either on paper or using computers.

> **Differentiation**
> **For older/more able children:** Invite the children to write a 'symptom sorter' list: 'To check if you have the dreaded shrinks'.
> **For younger/less able children:** Ask the children to draw and label a diagram showing how the stick will grow longer.

Get writing

Sensational scoop

> **Objective:** To write newspaper style reports.
> **What you need:** Copies of *The Twits*, flipchart, paper, writing materials.
> **Cross-curricular links:** ICT.

What to do

- Use this activity when the children have finished reading the book.
- Ask them to re-read the very last paragraph and imagine that a local newspaper ran an article about the Twits' disappearance.
- Brainstorm ideas for a newspaper headline, for example: 'Meter-reader Fred opens door on mystery' and, 'Tricksters' final vanishing act'.
- Ask who might be interviewed for their opinions and observations. Note ideas on a flipchart. Ask the children, in groups, to spend a few minutes inventing quotations from different people, for example: 'Every Wednesday a weird smell came from their kitchen.' Add suggestions to the flipchart.

- Start a class list of useful journalistic words and phrases: emotive tag words ('confessed'; 'admitted'); use of the passive tense ('It is alleged…'), and generalisations ('Police reveal…'), inviting the children to suggest more.
- Ask the children to write news reports about the episode, containing some 'true facts', as well as some inaccuracies, exaggerations and conjecture.
- Invite the children to read their reports to the group. Discuss how and where they are a mixture of truth and falsehood.

> **Differentiation**
> **For older/more able children:** Encourage the children to transfer their report to computer with an appropriate layout.
> **For younger/less able children:** Help the children create a list of true and false statements to incorporate into their report.

A new character

> **Objective:** To write character sketches, in the manner of the writer.
> **What you need:** Copies of *The Twits*, writing materials, photocopiable page 28, enlarged copy of Extract 1 (page 8).

What to do

- Use this activity once the children know enough about the two main characters to recognise their personalities. You may wish to spread this over more than one lesson.
- Look together at Extract 1. Identify what the reader learns about the characters and how. For example, physical descriptions of the Twits; direct speech, showing the kind of language they use and hinting at their relationship; their thought processes/methods of deceit; clues as to their preoccupations and interests.
- Ask the children to re-read the introductory

chapters of the book, making notes of how Dahl writes, his style – often addressing the reader, informal language, details of the characters' past. Mention also the importance of the Twits' name.

- Hand out the photocopiable sheet. Ask the children to plan a new unpleasant character, putting them in an opening situation which helps reveal more about them and their attitudes. Clarify that this is a brand new character for a brand new story.
- Encourage the children to write an opening paragraph, trying to make their readers dislike their new character.

> **Differentiation**
> **For older/more able children:** Challenge the children to plan chapters to create a complete story plan.
> **For younger/less able children:** Encourage the children to describe their character to a friend.

Get writing

Roly-Poly Bird's words

Objective: To write poetry based on the structure and/or style of poems read.
What you need: Copies of *The Twits*, enlarged copies of Extracts 1 and 3 (pages 8 and 10), flipchart, photocopiable page 29, paper, writing materials.

What to do
● Read Extract 3 together and identify the non-prose text. Note the AA/BB rhyme pattern. Highlight repetition and internal rhymes.
● Ask the children to look up Roly-Poly Bird's previous verse (at the end of 'The Roly-Poly Bird to the Rescue'). Can the children say which words change? (The ends of each of the lines.)
● Suggest that the Roly-Poly Bird might take pity on either Mr Twit or Mrs Twit during a trick. (Discuss briefly why this is unlikely!)
● Read Extract 1. Tell the children you want

them to invent a verse for the Roly-Poly Bird to warn Mr Twit about the glass eye in his beer.
● Create a rhyme word bank. Divide the children into six groups, asking each group to find rhymes for one of the following words: 'beer', 'glass', 'eye', 'shock', 'beware', 'drink'.
● Listen to the children's lists, noting possible words on the flipchart, such as: clear, fear and jeer.
● Remind the children that line ends must rhyme. Together, draft suggestions. Then, challenge the children to redraft for improvements.

Differentiation
For older/more able children: Ask the children individually to invent a warning verse about another trick.
For younger/less able children: Use photocopiable page 29 to help the children write a verse.

An alternative ending

Objective: To write an alternative ending and discuss how this would change the readers' view of the characters.
What you need: Copies of *The Twits*, flipchart and pen, photocopiable page 30, writing materials.
Cross-curricular links: Citizenship.

What to do
● This activity can be used alone or to follow on from the activity 'Baked in a pie' on page 21.
● Re-read the last chapter of the book.
● Discuss the ending. Is it satisfying? Is it fair? Ask the children how else the story might have ended. How could the author have changed the reader's opinion of the Twits? Might they learn to be reformed characters?
● Brainstorm how the Twits might have been saved. And by whom? (Each other; Fred; the Roly-Poly Bird; Muggle-Wump.)
● Invite suggestions as to how the Twits might

make amends. (For example, creating a bird and monkey sanctuary or planting live trees.) Record ideas on a flipchart.
● Ask the children to use the photocopiable sheet to plan a revised ending or additional chapter.
● Suggest that, to retain plausibility, the Twits would not entirely change. Mr Twit might shave his beard off, but still play tricks; the Twits might start eating Snail Pie instead of Bird Pie.
● Encourage the children to discuss ideas in pairs before writing their alternative ending.
● Once written encourage the children to share their endings with one another.

Differentiation
For older/more able children: Ask the children to include time phrases in their writing, drawing on examples from the book.
For younger/less able children: Discuss the characters' and the reader's feelings at the end of the book and what could change these.

Get writing

A new character

Choose a new character's name or invent one of your own:

Mr Bighead	Mrs Frown	Ms Hotfoot	Mr Whiff	

This is the face that my character sees when he or she looks in the mirror.

He/she is always saying things like this!

Appearance: _____

_____

including their most noticeable feature: _____

Something from their past (such as the worst thing they ever did):

_____

_____

A problem they have: _____

_____

A nasty habit: _____

_____

Where and how they live: _____

_____

_____

Where they are when the story begins: _____

_____

What they are doing: _____

_____

Get writing

Roly-Poly Bird's words

Re-read the chapter about the wormy spaghetti.
Look at these rhymes and add more of your own.

worms	plate	trick	wife	cheese
squirms	wait			

Write a song for the Roly-Poly Bird to sing
to warn Mr Twit not to eat his spaghetti.

Illustration © Quentin Blake

Begin with one of these lines or make up your own:

Beware of the meal prepared by your wife…
Look at the spaghetti, look close at your plate…
Watch out, Mr Twit, your wife's played a trick…

_____

_____

_____

_____

Use the other side of the sheet to make notes if you need to.

An alternative ending

Who helps save the Twits?

How?

Why?

Are the Twits grateful?

How do they show they are sorry to the birds and the monkeys?

Do they mean to behave better or have they been forced into it?

In what ways are the Twits different?

In what ways are they the same?

My new ending will be:

Assessment

Assessment advice

Readers of Roald Dahl's books are left in no doubt as to the author's opinions and where his sympathies lie. Often these are made clear when the author addresses the reader directly. Equally, they are apparent through the punishing outcomes of characters' reprehensible behaviour.

The Twits is a typical story from this author. Roald Dahl creates prejudices in the minds of his readers and then confirms these in the increasingly bizarre storyline. However, he provides explanations and exceptions – for instance, allowing that Mrs Twit's hideous looks are only a result of her unpleasant character.

Recognising that Roald Dahl wins his readers' sympathies, to be in line with his own, in order to gloat with him over the 'bad' characters' downfall and the victory of the 'good' underdog,

is essential to understanding the 'revenge' theme of this book. Much of his characterisation is achieved through creating stereotypes.

All novels need some characters, or aspects of characters, with which the reader can identify. We have to care about the characters to want to finish the book. A general class discussion about how and why the children like some characters and dislike others, want some to succeed and others to fail is a useful way of encouraging them to think about how an author can manipulate the reader and examine how the author's words and style have influenced their opinions.

Observe the children's responses during the course of the discussion. Invite children to challenge if they disagree, or to explain why they do agree with points made.

Using stereotypes

> **Assessment focus:** To identify stereotypical characters and evaluate their behaviour, through recall of significant events in *The Twits*.
> **What you need:** Copies of *The Twits*, photocopiable page 32, writing materials.

What to do
- Sum up the children's findings from the class discussion on why the children like or dislike characters, as described above.
- Explain that Roald Dahl *tells* and *shows* us what to think about characters, situations and behaviour. He makes us look at things through his eyes and encourages us to agree with him.
- Point out that characters behaving exactly how we expect them to behave are called stereotypes. Give examples (such as a crying baby).

- Explain that stereotypical fictional characters, behaviour and situations live up to their image. They often verify sayings and maxims – such as: 'Pride comes before a fall' or, 'Absence makes the heart grow fonder'.
- Hand out a copy of photocopiable page 32 to each child. Ask the children to find examples of events that verify the quoted maxims.
- Expect answers along the lines of: the monkeys get rid of both Twits with one trick; incident of trespassing boys; 'payback' tricks – large or small; Twits show fear when they are at risk; what the Twits say and do are not the same (spaghetti; floating up); Roly-Poly Bird's role; the determination, plan and execution of the monkeys in turning the house upside down.
- As a class, discuss the findings for each sayin in turn.

Using stereotypes

The behaviour of stereotypical characters can often be summed up through old sayings.

Find examples from *The Twits* that verify the sayings in the table below.

Illustration © Quentin Blake

Traditional old saying	How and where do the characters and their behaviour prove the old sayings true?
● Any port in a storm	Mrs Twit turns to Mr Twit for help and advice when she is panicked into thinking that she is shrinking. Even though she knows he tricks her, she has no one else to help.
● Kill two birds with one stone	
● Tit for tat is fair play	
● Bullies are generally cowards	
● As you sow, so shall you reap	

Roald Dahl's book, *The Twits*, is a story of revenge.
Explain in your own words how this is true on the reverse side of this page.